FIRSTS and Almost Firsts IN HAWAI'I

FIRSTS *and Almost Firsts*
IN
HAWAI'I

Compiled by Robert C. Schmitt

Edited by Ronn Ronck

A Kolowalu Book
University of Hawai'i Press
Honolulu

Library of Congress Cataloging-in-Publication Data
Schmitt, Robert C.
    Firsts and almost firsts in Hawai'i / Robert C. Schmitt, Ronn Ronck.
        p.   cm.   (A Kolowalu book)
    Includes bibliographical references.
    ISBN 0-8248-1282-4 (acid-free paper)
    1. Hawaii--Miscellanea.   I. Ronck, Ronn.   II. Title.
DU623.S36   1995
996.9--dc20   95-24713
                                                              CIP

Publishing coordination and book production by
Laing Communications Inc., Redmond, Washington, and Edmonton, Alberta

Design, Illustration and Production: Sandra J. Harner
Editorial Coordination/Copyediting: Susan B. Bureau and Lori Ljubicich
Original scratch board art © 1995 Laing Communications Inc.

Contents

Alphabetical List of "Firsts"

*The following is an alphabetical listing of
all the "firsts" covered in this book.*

Reference Abbreviations

The following abbreviations are used in the notes at the end of each "first" entry. For information on additional resources, see References on page 231.

A	*Aloha*
ABCFM	American Board of Commissioners for Foreign Missions
AH	State Archives of Hawaii
DB	*Daily Bulletin*
EB	*The Evening Bulletin*
F	*The Friend*
H	*Honolulu*
HA	*The Honolulu Advertiser*
HAA	*Hawaiian Almanac and Annual* (Thrum's Almanac)
HD	*Hawaiian Digest*
HG	*The Hawaiian Gazette*
HHN	*Historic Hawaii News*
HHR	*Hawaii Historical Review*
HHS	Hawaiian Historical Society
HJH	*Hawaiian Journal of History*
HMCS	Hawaiian Mission Children's Society
HMJ	*Hawaii Medical Journal*
HRS	Hawaii Revised Statutes
HS	*The Hawaiian Star*
HSB	*Honolulu Star-Bulletin*
MH	*Missionary Herald*
P	*The Polynesian*
PBN	*Pacific Business News*
PCA	*Pacific Commercial Advertiser*
PP	*Paradise of the Pacific*
RLH	Revised Laws of Hawaii

SHDB	*The State of Hawaii Data Book*
SIG	*Sandwich Island Gazette*
SIM	*Sandwich Island Mirror and Commercial Gazette*
SIN	*Sandwich Island News*
SLH	Session Laws of Hawaii
SSB&A	*Sunday Star-Bulletin and Advertiser*

Acknowledgments

The authors would like to express their sincere gratitude to those who have made important contributions to *Firsts and Almost Firsts in Hawai'i*. At the top of the list is the staff of the University of Hawai'i Press—especially William Hamilton and Iris Wiley—who encouraged and supported this project from beginning to end. Cindy Cordes typed the original manuscript, helped shape the material, and provided valuable insight. Bob Krauss of *The Honolulu Advertiser* generously shared discoveries from his own historical research and introduced us to many new "firsts." The staffs of the Hawaii State Archives and Hawaii State Library also helped with documentation. Special thanks are extended to the Hawaiian Historical Society and its *Hawaiian Journal of History*, where much of the information in these pages first appeared.

Introduction

The 1909 issue of Thomas George Thrum's Hawaiian Almanac and Annual carried an unsigned article titled, "A Chapter of Firstlings." The piece was likely authored by Thrum himself, who had first published his periodical (popularly called "Thrum's Almanac") in 1875 and continued doing so until his death in 1932.

In the article's thirteen pages, Thrum listed 136 important Hawai'i introductions, ranging from agricultural implements to whaling ships. He also included the first centipede, first elephant, first Pali road, first fire engine, first sewing machine, and first smallpox epidemic, among other items.

Unfortunately, Thrum's article can no longer be viewed as definitive. Many introductions have taken place since it was written in 1908, and many earlier "firsts," unmentioned by Thrum, are worth recording. Furthermore, several of the dates he cited were up to nine years off the mark.

In 1962, Katherine D. McDole privately printed a little known update of Thrum's work, *Iamu I Hiki Ai* (It happened here in Hawaii). It included 185 references, but seventeen contained inaccuracies. Neither Thrum's nor McDole's efforts included any documentation for the dates and events listed. Consequently, we felt that a revised, updated, and properly documented book of firsts was in order.

Such an undertaking inevitably generates some difficulties.

Comprehensiveness is an unattainable ideal. Some events of unquestioned significance in Island history seem to have gone unrecorded, while others, interesting only to the most devoted trivia buffs, are available in profusion.

Many firsts, too, can be infinitely subdivided. Where should one stop? Then there is the question of conflicting dates. Standard reference works—even the most reputable—are strewn with inaccuracies.

Firsts and Almost Firsts in Hawai'i is by necessity highly selective. Some subjects, fully and accurately treated in the Thrum and McDole lists, are mentioned only briefly or not at all. Other subjects, omitted by earlier authors or misdated in the past, have been covered in greater detail.

Introductions to Hawai'i, of course, will never end, and the process of documenting them will continue after *Firsts and Almost Firsts in Hawai'i* is in the hands of readers. We encourage readers to bring to our attention any additions for possible inclusion in subsequent editions.

Island Residents

Anthropology and Archaeology

The officers and crew of Captain James Cook's third voyage recorded the earliest anthropological observations of Hawaiians in 1778 and 1779.

In 1841, the Wilkes Expedition visited the Ahu o 'Umi. The expedition's plan of this ancient *heiau* is probably the earliest scientific map of a Hawaiian archaeological site.

John F. G. Stokes, curator of ethnology for the Bernice Pauahi Bishop Museum, has been called the first Hawaiian archaeologist. In 1913, he became the first to conduct a systematic subsurface excavation at a prehistoric Hawaiian site, on the island of Kahoʻolawe.

The first radiocarbon date for any island in the Pacific was A.D. 1004, plus or minus about 180 years. Kenneth Emory and his students excavated the sample of charcoal used in the calculation from the lowest level of a fireplace in a rock shelter in Kuli'ou'ou, O'ahu, in May 1950.

Kirch (1985): 9–11, 15–16; Krauss (1988): 322–324, 338.

Beachboys

Early in 1897, a group of native canoe owners in Waikīkī formed an organization, the Hui Pakaka Nalu, to offer outrigger canoe rides through the surf to tourists for one dollar per person per hour. As many as eight canoes were reported in operation at peak periods. The *hui* was the first formal organization of beachboys.

PCA, 10 May 1897, 2; PCA, 18 May 1897, 7; PCA, 25 May 1897, 7; PCA, 31 May 1897, 6; HA, 14 Dec. 1989, A13.

Blacks

Blacks first sailed to the Islands as crew members of merchant ships in the early nineteenth century. Some remained behind and settled in the Islands. One of the earliest businessmen in Hawai'i was Anthony D. Allen, a black man from New York, who was an Island resident by 1810.

The first black contract laborers arrived January 2, 1901, most of them destined for work on Maui plantations.

By 1990, there were 27,195 blacks living in Hawai'i. Almost 65 percent were members of the armed forces or military dependents.

HJH (1988): 241–255; U.S. House Committee on Immigration and Naturalization, *Labor Problems in Hawaii, Hearings on H. J. Res. 158 . . . and H. J. Res. 171. . .*, 67th Cong., 1st sess. (1921): 539; SHDB 1992: 44; Hawaii State Dept. of Business, Economic Development & Tourism, Statistical Report 227, Dec. 1993, table 5.

Chinese

The first Chinese known to have visited Hawai'i were members of the crew of the *Felice*, under Captain John Meares. Outfitted in China and crewed by fifty Chinese, the ship berthed in Hawai'i for eight days in 1788 on its way back to China from the Pacific Northwest.

Chinese became Island residents soon afterward. Edward Bell, who arrived with Captain George Vancouver in 1794, observed Chinese among the foreigners in Kamehameha's retinue at Kealakekua Bay.

The Chinese community remained small until 1852, when the first Chinese contract laborers arrived. Thereafter, their members grew rapidly, from 364 in 1853 to 25,767 in 1900 and 68,804 (including some but not all persons of part-Chinese blood) in 1990.

Lum (1988): 10–11; *Report of the President of the Bureau of Immigration to the Legislative Assembly of 1886*: 266–277; Schmitt (1977): 25–26, 97–98, 100–103; *SHDB 1992*: 44.

Contract Labor

"An Act for the Government of Masters and Servants," passed by the legislature in 1850, provided the legal basis for the contract labor system that existed in Hawai'i throughout the second half of the nineteenth century and brought many thousands of workers to toil on the major plantations. The act made it lawful for any person over twenty years of age to bind himself "by written contract to serve another in any . . . employment" for up to five years.

The first contract laborers brought to Hawai'i were 195 Chinese men who arrived from Hong Kong aboard the *Thetis* on January 3, 1852.

Later groups who came to work in the sugar and pineapple plantations included South Sea Islanders (initially in 1859 and 1865), Japanese (first in 1868), Portuguese (1878), Norwegians (1881), Germans (1881), Puerto Ricans (1900), Koreans (1903), Filipinos (1906), and Spaniards (1907). Although the Masters and Servants Act expired after Hawai'i was annexed to the United States, the importation of plantation labor continued until 1946.

Kuykendall (1938): 330; *Report of the President of the Bureau of Immigration to the Legislative Assembly of 1886*: 266–277; U.S. House Committee on Immigration and Naturalization, *Labor Problems in Hawaii, Hearings on H. J. Res. 158 . . . and H. J. Res. 171 . . .*, 67th Cong., 1st sess. (1921): 533–545; Nordyke (1989): 30, 32–33, 35, 41, 45, 47.

Filipinos

It is not known when the first Filipinos came to Hawai'i. The earliest statistical record appeared in the 1853 census, which reported five persons from the Philippines living in Hawai'i.

The first Filipino contract workers—fifteen men—arrived on the SS *Doric* on December 20, 1906. Their numbers increased rapidly during the following quarter of a century, from 2,361 in 1910 to 63,052 in 1930 and 168,682 (many of mixed blood) in 1990.

Schmitt (1977): 25–26, 90–91; Dorita (1975): 7; *SHDB 1992*: 44.

Hawaiians

The first Hawaiians are thought to have been Polynesians from the Marquesas Islands who reached Hawai'i sometime between A.D. 300 and 600.

Their population slowly increased over the centuries; by the time of Captain James Cook's visit in 1778, it probably exceeded a quarter of a million. Other authorities have proposed pre-contact figures ranging from 100,000 to more than 800,000.

Whatever the 1778 population, it rapidly declined, and by 1910, only 26,041 Hawaiians and 12,506 part-Hawaiians lived on the Islands.

Official estimates for 1989, based on a survey by the Department of Health, reported 8,843 Hawaiians and 198,147 part-Hawaiians. The 1990 census count of 138,742 "Hawaiians" included some but not all part-Hawaiians.

Kirch (1985): 286, 298, 302, 304; Schmitt (1977): 7, 25–26; Stannard (1989); *SHDB 1992*: 42, 44; *New Zealand J. Archaeology* 14 (1992): 113–128.

Japanese

The first Japanese to visit Hawai'i were drifting or shipwrecked seamen. Although some historians claim visits going back to the thirteenth century, the earliest documented arrival occurred in 1804, when a Russian vessel picked up four survivors and put them ashore in Hawai'i.

The first Japanese contract workers were 142 men and six women who arrived aboard the *Scioto* in 1868.

The Japanese population rose from 116 in 1884 to 61,111 in 1900, 184,598 in 1950, and 247,486 (some of mixed blood) in 1990.

United Japanese Society of Hawaii (1971): 5–8; *Report of the President of the Bureau of Immigration to the Legislative Assembly of 1886*: 266–277; Schmitt (1977): 25–26; *SHDB 1992*: 44.

Koreans

The first Koreans to establish residence in Hawai'i were two ginseng merchants who arrived in 1896.

The first Korean contract laborers consisted of fifty-six men (two of them interpreters), twenty-one women, thirteen children, and twelve infants, who came to Honolulu aboard the *Gaelic* on January 13, 1903.

The Korean population reached 4,533 in 1910, 7,030 in 1950, and 24,454 (many of mixed blood) in 1990.

Patterson (1988): 9–11, 49–51; Schmitt (1977): 25–26; *SHDB 1992*: 44.

Portuguese

Hawai'i's pioneer Portuguese settlers arrived early in the nineteenth century, appearing in census tabulations as early as 1853.

Portuguese contract workers first arrived aboard the *Priscilla*, from Madeira, Portugal, on September 30, 1878. This group included eighty men, forty women, and sixty children.

The Portuguese population rose from ninety in 1866 to 18,272 in 1900 and 27,588 in 1930. In 1990, the census reported 57,125 persons of Portuguese ancestry living in the state.

Schmitt (1977): 25–26, 90–91; *Report of the President of the Bureau of Immigration to the Legislative Assembly of 1886*: 266–277; U.S. House Committee on Immigration and Naturalization, *Labor Problems in Hawaii, Hearings on H. J. Res. 158 . . . and H. J. Res. 17 . . .*, 67th Cong., 1st sess. (1921): 538; *SHDB 1992*: 45.

Puerto Ricans

Hawai'i's earliest Puerto Rican residents were fifty-six contract laborers who arrived on the SS *City of Rio de Janeiro* on December 23, 1900.

The Puerto Rican population grew to 4,890 in 1910 and 9,551 in 1950. By 1990, 16,432 residents of Hawai'i claimed Puerto Rican ancestry.

Carr (1980): 9; Schmitt (1977): 25–26; *SHDB 1992*: 45.

Samoans

Hawai'i's earliest Samoan residents were apparently Mormons who settled at Lā'ie, on O'ahu, after the Mormon Temple was completed there in 1919. By 1990, there were 14,073 Samoans in Hawai'i.

HHR, July 1968, 455–459; *SHDB 1992*: 44.

Whites

The first white resident of Hawai'i was John Mackay (or McKey), who arrived on the *Imperial Eagle* in May 1787.

Frances Hornsby Trevor Barkley was probably the first European woman to visit Hawai'i. She also arrived aboard the *Imperial Eagle* in 1787. The ship took away the first Hawaiian known to sail for foreign lands—a woman hired to be Barkley's maid. Her name was listed as "Wynee," which may have been an attempt to spell the Hawaiian word *wahine*, or woman.

The 1990 white population was 369,616, of whom 20.9 percent were either military personnel or their dependents; many persons classified as white in the decennial census were racially mixed.

Day (1984): 8, 91; *SHDB 1992*: 44; Hawaii State Dept. of Business, Economic Development & Tourism, Statistical Report 227, Dec. 1993, table 5.

Birds and Beasts

Alligators

The Islands' first resident alligator—a female named Arabella—accompanied Brother Matthias Newell when he came from New Orleans in 1886 to join the Brothers of Mary at St. Louis College, then located on College Walk. Only seven inches long when she arrived (in a cigar box), Arabella eventually reached a length of more than six feet. She remained at St. Louis for more than twenty years and, after her death, was stuffed and put on exhibition.

HSB, 23 Sept. 1983, B1.

Birds

One of the earliest birds deliberately introduced to the Islands was the spotted, lace-necked, or Chinese dove, although the exact year is unknown.

In 1865, Dr. William Hillebrand brought the common mynah from India to combat the army worms ravaging Island pasture lands. Hillebrand also brought the spotted munia, or ricebird.

Imported from New Zealand, the house sparrow (or English sparrow) was released in Honolulu in 1871.

The rock dove, a variety of the common pigeon and a descendant of the European rock dove, was introduced to Hawai'i in 1896.

The first barred doves came to the Islands from Malaysia sometime after 1922.

The red-crested (or Brazilian) cardinal was first released on O'ahu in 1928. The Kentucky (or Virginia) cardinal was released between 1929 and 1931.

The Territorial Board of Agriculture and Forestry brought the Japanese white-eye from Japan in 1929 and subsequently released it on O'ahu.

The cattle egret was imported from Florida to help control house flies, horn flies, and other flies that damaged hides and reduced weight gain in cattle. More than one hundred cattle egrets were released on five islands between July 17 and August 24, 1959.

Berger (1981): 175, 178, 179, 198, 203, 210, 214, 216, 219.

Cattle

During his second voyage, in 1793, Captain George Vancouver brought the first cattle to Hawai'i. Five cows, two of them in calf, were brought ashore in Kamehameha's canoes at Kealakekua Bay on February 22. These animals, acquired by Vancouver at Mission San Carlos, near Monterey, California, were later joined by additional cattle transported aboard his third voyage, in 1794. All of the cattle thrived in the Islands.

Tomich (1986): 141–142.

Deer

Eight axis deer were released on Moloka'i in January 1868. The descendants of this herd still live on the island.

Tomich (1986): 126–127.

Dog Shows

The Hawaiian Kennel Club held the first dog show in the Islands on September 6, 7, and 8, 1906, in a building at Queen and Edinburgh Streets in Honolulu. J. L. Fleming's pointer, Tess, won first prize over 104 other entries.

PP, Sept. 1906, 8.

Donkeys

Richard Charlton, the first British consul to Hawai'i, imported four donkeys in 1825 and later sold them at auction in Honolulu.

Tomich (1986): 114–115.

Frogs

The Royal Agricultural Society brought the first frogs to Hawai'i sometime before 1867. The earliest recorded shipment, however, occurred in 1867, when "frogs were liberated at Pawaa" in Honolulu.

Bryan (1915): 297.

Goats

On February 2, 1778, Captain James Cook left behind Hawai'i's first three goats—a ram and two ewes—during his visit to Ni'ihau.

Tomich (1986): 151.

Horses and Horse Racing

Horses were first brought to Hawai'i in 1803, aboard a merchant ship under the command of Captain William Shaler. Shaler and his partner, R. J. Cleveland, brought ashore a mare at "Tooagah" Bay and a mare and a stallion on Maui. The horses "excited great astonishment among the natives," Cleveland reported. But horses soon became common, and in 1832, the first of the Mexican cowboys, or *paniolos*, arrived at Waimea, on the Big Island.

Horse racing was initially quite informal, involving only two animals at a time on courses in open areas or along public roads. During the 1840s, horseback riding became popular, and horse racing was common along Wilder Avenue. In the 1850s, Sunday afternoon contests were held, pitting fast studs from California against wiry, grass-fed O'ahu mustangs. Bets ranged from "one bit" to fifty dollars.

Regularly scheduled racing eventually took place on permanent oval tracks. Kamehameha Day, first celebrated on June 11, 1872, was marked by racing on "The Plains." In 1877, the Kamehameha Day races were moved to the one-mile circular course at the newly opened Kapi'olani Park, where they became a regular attraction for many years.

Tomich (1986): 110–111; *HAA 1939*: 105; Scott (1968): 59, 69, 650; *PP*, June 1903, 11–12; Hibbard and Franzen (1986): 42–43.

Mongooses

The small Indian mongoose was introduced to Hawai'i in the 1860s. In 1883, seventy-two mongooses were brought to the Islands and released on the Hilo and Hāmākua coasts.

Tomich (1986): 95–96.

Sheep

Domestic sheep were introduced by Captain James Colnett of the *Argonaut*, a merchant ship en route from the Pacific coast of North America. Colnett brought a ram and two ewes to Kaua'i in April 1791. Captain George Vancouver put a ram, two ewes, and a lamb ashore at Kawaihae on the Big Island, on February 14, 1793.

Tomich (1986): 158.

Snakes

The only land snake to be found in the wild in Hawai'i is the tiny Hawaiian blind snake. This wormlike creature is thought to have arrived in soil surrounding plants brought from the Philippines in 1929 to landscape the Kamehameha School grounds.

McKeown (1978): 9, 59.

Toads

In April 1932, at the request of the Hawaiian Sugar Planters' Association, C. E. Pemberton introduced 147 or 148 giant neotropical toads to O'ahu to control sugarcane beetles. The toads were from Puerto Rico, where they had successfully battled cane field pests. Lacking natural predators in Hawai'i, they numbered more than a million only two and a half years after their arrival. (See also *Frogs*.)

McKeown (1978): 6, 20–21; HSB, 6 Oct. 1934, sec. 3, p. 1.

Insects and Arthropods

Bees

A 1931 study noted that more than sixty species of bees lived in the Hawaiian Islands, at least three-quarters of which could be found nowhere else in the world.

In 1848, a newspaper editor reported: "A bumble-bee visited our office a few days since. They made their appearance in Lahaina about two years since, but we have never heard of their being seen in this island [Oʻahu] before."

Honey bees were imported in both 1853 and 1857. On August 1, 1853, the bark *Matanzas* arrived in Honolulu with a hive of bees from Boston. Only a few bees were still alive, however, and these survived only a short time. Four years later, a shipment of honey bees arrived from San Jose, California, and survived.

The commercial production of honey and beeswax dates from 1893. In that year, St. John Gilbert and his brother captured a stray swarm of bees in their Honolulu garden and began the Sandwich Island Honey Company. In 1894, they shipped eight gallons of honey to the United States. Production increased rapidly after this modest start and by World War II reached 1,000,000 pounds of extracted or liquid honey, 10,000 pounds of wax, and 5,000 pounds of comb honey.

Williams (1931): 228; P, 14 Oct. 1848, 87; P, 14 May 1853, 2; P, 6 Aug. 1853, 50; HA, 21 Oct. 1978, A3; W. D. Alexander (1899): 335; Degener (1946): sheet 169a; Eckert (1951): 1; PP, Dec. 1942, 17–21; Philipp (1953): 50.

Butterflies

Butterflies and moths arrived soon after Captain James Cook's visits. The first species of *Lepidoptera* recorded in Hawai'i was King Kamehameha's butterfly, which was described in 1821 from specimens collected from 1815 to 1818. The first moths were collected from 1825 to 1828.

Zimmerman (1958): 23.

Centipedes

Large centipedes (six or more inches in length) were introduced in either 1829 or 1836. At least one smaller species has been brought in since that time.

Bryan (1915): 407; Williams (1931): 313, 317; Barrot (1978): 72. The 1829 date is Barrot's; Bryan's was 1836.

Centipedes, Scolopendra subspinipes, *were first recorded in Hawai'i in 1829 or 1836.* Sketch from David T. Fullaway and Noel L. H. Krauss, Common Insects of Hawaii (1945).

Cockroaches

The first cockroach recorded by species name was the burrowing, Surinam, or bicolored cockroach in 1822. The Madera cockroach, the largest cockroach currently found in the Islands (up to fifty millimeters long), was initially observed in 1896 or 1897. The American cockroach was first noted in 1882, the German and Australian cockroaches in 1899, and the brown-banded cockroach in 1921. By 1948, eighteen species in fifteen genera were found in the Islands, all of them introduced since 1778.

Zimmerman (1948): 77, 84, 88, 91–94.

Fleas

Fleas (*'uku*) were probably brought to Hawai'i by the early settlers. One flea is known to be a parasite of the Polynesian rat.

More aggressive varieties of fleas were introduced by European or American ships sometime before 1809. Called *'ukulele* (leaping flea) by the Hawaiians, they soon infested huts, caves, and interisland schooners.

Hardy (1960): 17; HJH (1971): 59–74.

Fruit Flies

In 1895, the melon fly was accidentally introduced from the Orient and was soon regarded the most destructive pest of vegetable crops in the Islands. The Mediterranean fruit fly reached Hawai'i from Australia about 1907 and quickly became a notorious hazard to soft-pulped fruits. Late in World War II, the Oriental fruit fly arrived, apparently from Saipan, and replaced the Mediterranean fruit fly in lowland areas. The Oriental fruit fly attacks almost all kinds of fruits and vegetables.

Hardy (1960): 23–24.

Mosquitoes

Night-biting mosquitoes were imported in water casks on ships from Mexico between 1826 and 1830. Two types of day-biting mosquitoes arrived later and were common by the 1890s.

Hardy (1960): 18–20. Barrot (1978): 72. Barrot dated the first mosquito in 1822.

Scorpions

Scorpions were first recorded in Hawai'i in 1829.

Barrot (1978): 72.

Termites

All four of the termites found in the Islands are immigrants. Hawai'i's earliest arrival, evidently before 1869, was the dry-wood termite. The lowland-tree termite and forest-tree termite were first recorded in 1883. A subterranean termite was discovered in 1907 or earlier.

Zimmerman (1948): 159, 165, 169, 171–172.

Vegetation and Crops

Algaroba Trees

All of Hawai'i's algaroba (or *kiawe*) trees came from a seed brought to the Islands in 1827 and planted by Father Alexis Bachelot in 1828 in the Catholic Mission grounds on Fort Street in Honolulu. The seed derived from a Chilean tree growing in the Jardin du Roi in Paris.

Degener (1946): sheet 169a; *HAA 1920*: 157; *18th Annual Report, HHS, 1910*: 29–34; *HSB*, 16 Nov. 1982, A12; *HSB*, 2 June 1978, D9.

Anthuriums

Samuel Mills Damon brought the first anthurium plants to Hawai'i from London in 1889.

Neal (1965): 134; *HSB*, 16 Nov. 1982, A13.

Avocados

Don Francisco de Paula Marin gets credit for introducing the avocado or alligator pear to Hawai'i in the early nineteenth century, according to records of the Royal Agricultural Society.

Degener (1946): sheet 137.

Bananas

Wild or native bananas were brought to Hawai'i by early Polynesian settlers. General William Miller brought the Chinese banana from Tahiti in 1855. The Bluefield banana was introduced in 1903.

Degener (1945): 109; Bryan (1915): 257, 259–260; HSB, 16 Nov. 1982, A13.

Carnations

In October 1878, Emma Louise Dillingham apparently brought the first carnation plant to Hawai'i from California.

Frear (1934): 265.

Coffee

According to botanist Otto Degener, Arabian coffee must have been brought to the Islands before December 30, 1817, because Don Francisco de Paula Marin wrote in his journal that he planted it that day. These plants apparently died soon afterward.

Coffee was reintroduced eight years later by John Wilkinson, who gathered the plants in Rio de Janeiro, Brazil, and planted them on Governor Boki's plantation in Mānoa in 1825.

Degener (1945): 276–277.

Eucalyptuses

Around 1867, H. Holstein imported the first eucalyptus seed from Sydney, Australia, for Captain James Makee.

PCA, 3 Apr. 1875, 3.

Guavas

Hawai'i's common guava is thought to have first been planted by Don Francisco de Paula Marin, who lived in the Islands from 1793 to 1837. The actual date of planting, however, is unknown.

Degener (1945): 228; Neal (1965): 632.

Hibiscus

A number of species of hibiscus grow in Hawai'i, some native and some introduced. The exact date of introduction of non-native species is unknown, but the earliest recorded mention dates to 1854—a reference to the *Hibiscus rosa sinensis*, a red flower from China sometimes called the shoe black flower.

HAA 1918: 87; HSB, 3 Sept. 1990, B1.

Ironwood Trees

A man named Isenberg planted the first ironwood trees (*Casuarina*) at Kilohana Crater, Kaua'i, in 1882.

Neal (1965): 289.

Macadamia Nuts

Macadamia nuts were first brought to Hawai'i from their native Australia around 1881, when William Herbert Purvis, who managed the Pacific Sugar Mill at Kukuihaele on the Big Island, planted seed nuts at Kapulena.

In 1892, a decade after Purvis' initial planting, the Jordan brothers, Edward Walter and Robert Alfred, successfully planted some seeds at Edward's home on Wyllie Street in Nuʻuanu. Additional macadamia nut trees were planted by the Hawaiian government on the slopes of Tantalus as part of a reforestation project between 1892 and 1894.

Commercial planting began much later. In 1921, Ernest Shelton Van Tassel leased seventy-five acres of government land on Round Top and planted seeds from the Jordan and Purvis trees. On June 1, 1922, Van Tassel formed the Hawaiian Macadamia Nut Company, Ltd. Other planters quickly followed, establishing nut farms on Oʻahu, the Big Island, and elsewhere.

In the fall of 1934, commercial processing of macadamia nuts began at Van Tassel's new factory at Keawe and Pohukaina Streets in Kakaʻako. The nuts were shelled, roasted, salted, bottled, and marketed under the increasingly popular brand name of Van's Macadamia Nuts.

Macadamia nut candies first became commercially available a few years later. Two well-known confectioners, Ellen Dye Candies at 1112 Fort Street and the Alexander Young Hotel candy shop at Bishop and Hotel Streets, began making and selling chocolate-covered macadamia nut candy sometime during the middle or late 1930s.

Shigeura and Ooka (1984): 5–7, 11–16; Nellist, ed. (1941): 721; HA, 13 Feb. 1938, 9; HSB, 19 Jan. 1935, 11; Hawaii Agricultural Experiment Station, Bull. No. 59 (1929): 21; Works Progress Administration (N.d.): 37, 339, 340, 345; Clara Orenstein (prewar Alexander Young employee), interview, 28 Aug. 1994; *Polk-Husted Directory Co.'s Directory of City and County of Honolulu . . . 1940–1941*: 244; HA 10 Dec. 1948, 3.

Mangos

The common mango was probably introduced by Don Francisco de Paula Marin from Mexico in the early 1800s, or by Captain John Meek in 1824. Marin planted a tree near Vineyard and River Streets in Honolulu.

S. M. Damon brought the Pirie or Paheri mango from India in 1899. The Haden variety came to Hawai'i from Florida around 1930.

Degener (1946): Book 5, sheet 196; Neal (1965): 521; HA, 10 May 1979, B1.

Marijuana

The earliest published reference to marijuana appears to be a January 1932 newspaper article reporting the recent appearance of the drug, shipped from mainland ports, and the fining of a Puerto Rican woman for possession and sale of marijuana cigarettes. No cannabis was found growing in the Islands until November 1937, when Manuel Vierra reported two large plants, both over eight feet high, growing in Pauoa Valley, Honolulu. Vierra had planted the seeds, received from a co-worker, ten months earlier under the impression that they were tobacco seeds.

HA, 6 Jan. 1932, 1–2; HSB, 13 Nov. 1937, 7; HSB, 23 Mar. 1979, A9.

Monkeypod Trees

The American consul P. A. Brinsmade introduced the monkeypod tree to Hawai'i when he brought two seeds from Mexico in 1847. They were planted in a garden near the site of the former Alexander Young Hotel. Both sprouted and soon had descendants on Kaua'i and elsewhere throughout the Kingdom.

HSB, 16 Nov. 1982, A12.

Oranges

Oranges were introduced by Captain George Vancouver in 1792. Before reaching Hawai'i, Vancouver and his men had visited Tahiti, where oranges were well established.

Bryan (1915): 263.

Papayas

Papayas grew in Hawai'i either before Captain James Cook arrived in 1778 or not long afterward. Today's commercial solo papaya, however, was developed from seeds that Gerrit P. Wilder sent from Barbados to J. E. Higgins of the Hawaii Agricultural Experiment Station in July 1911.

HSB, 16 Nov. 1982, A12, A13.

Passion Fruit

The passion fruit (liliko'i or purple granadilla) had arrived by 1888, when it was noted as growing wild in East Maui.

Degener (1946), sheet 250.

Pineapples

How the first pineapple came to Hawai'i is unknown, but Don Francisco de Paula Marin made the earliest recorded planting in 1813. By the middle of the century, thousands of fresh pineapples were shipped to California.

In 1885 and 1886, Captain John Kidwell imported the first Cayenne pineapple into Hawai'i. This variety soon became dominant in the Islands.

Pineapple canning was first tried in Hawai'i more than a century ago and exhibited at the 1876 Philadelphia Exposition. J. D. Ackerman and E. Muller attempted the first commercial canning in 1882 at Kona on the island of Hawai'i. They soon abandoned the venture, however, because of a lack of market response.

The modern pineapple industry dates from 1900, when a group of California farmers formed a colony at Wahiawā, O'ahu, and, under the leadership of Byron O. Clark, began raising a number of crops, including pineapples. In 1901, James D. Dole organized the Hawaiian Pineapple Company. His first crop, canned in 1903, amounted to 1,893 cases.

Kuykendall (1967): 108–109; Kuykendall and Day (1961): 236.

Poinciana Trees

Dr. William Hillebrand is thought to have introduced the royal poinciana tree about 1855.

Degener (1946): sheet 169b.

Royal Palm Trees

Dr. Gerrit P. Judd brought the seed for Hawai'i's first royal palm from Havana, Cuba, in 1850. He planted it at the corner of Bates Street and Nu'uanu Avenue, on a lot owned by his sister.

HSB, 16 Nov. 1982, A12.

Shower Trees

Shower trees were introduced to Hawai'i during the last half of the nineteenth century. The pink shower tree (*Cassia grandis*), the pink-and-white shower tree (*Cassia javanica*), and the golden shower tree (*Cassia fistula*) all were cultivated in Hawai'i as far back as 1870. Hybrids like the rainbow shower (*Cassia javanica* and *Cassia fistula*) soon followed.

The Honolulu Improvement Club, organized in 1905, planted numerous shower and poinciana trees along Wilder Avenue, Pensacola Street, and Pi'ikoi Street.

Degener (1946): family 169b; Neal (1965): 424; HA, 19 Mar. 1928, ed. p. [p. 10].

Tobacco

Tobacco cultivation dates at least to 1809, when Archibald Campbell observed that "smoking tobacco is another luxury of which the natives are very fond." Don Francisco de Paula Marin planted tobacco in 1813.

Six years later, the use of tobacco was widespread in the Sandwich Islands. Chieftains as well as their servants would pass a single pipe from one person to another.

The first systematic attempts at commercial tobacco cultivation occurred in Hanalei Valley, Kaua'i, in 1851, or possibly earlier.

Campbell (1967): 135; *HAA 1910*: 111–117; De Freycinet (1978): 64–65.

Weather and Geology

Hurricanes

Before 1950, several severe windstorms striking Hawai'i were described as hurricanes but are now regarded by meteorologists as probably Kona storms or other lesser events. One such "hurricane" devastated Lahaina, Maui, on February 15 and 16, 1850, killing five or six persons aboard the *Sophia*, destroying more than 100 homes (including the King's palace), and blowing down more than 5,000 banana trees.

The earliest blow in the historical record now thought to have been a true hurricane struck North and South Kohala on the Big Island and Lahaina on Maui on August 9, 1871, blowing down about 150 houses and causing damage estimated at $5,000.

The first named hurricane to reach Hawai'i—Hiki—struck on August 15 to 17, 1950. Damage was centered on Kaua'i, where sustained winds at Kilauea Lighthouse averaged sixty-eight miles per hour. One person died, and losses were estimated at $200,000.

Samuel L. Shaw, A History of Tropical Cyclones in the Central North Pacific and the Hawaiian Islands 1832–1979 (Silver Spring, Md., National Weather Service, Sept. 1981), 9, 15–18, 28–30; P, 23 Feb. 1850, 162; Hiki damage estimate by U. S. Geological Survey, cited by Robert T. Chuck, Div. of Land and Water Development, in letter to Schmitt, 5 Dec. 1983; discussions by Schmitt with Paul Haraguchi, Div. of Water and Land Development, 9 Feb. 1990, and Saul Price, National Weather Service, 13 Feb. 1990.

Maps

The earliest known charts of the Hawaiian Islands date from January or February 1778, soon after Captain James Cook's first landfall in the archipelago. One is the work of Thomas Edgar, master on the HMS *Discovery*; the other is the work of James Burney, first lieutenant on the same vessel. Both charts show Kaula, Ni'ihau, Kaua'i, and a piece of O'ahu in considerable detail.

The earliest published chart of the Hawaiian Islands was included in the official account of Cook's third voyage, issued in 1784. Drawn by Lieutenant Henry Roberts, the engraved chart depicts all eight major islands and includes a detailed inset showing Karakakooa [Kealakekua] Bay.

Otto von Kotzebue, captain of the Russian ship *Rurik*, drew the earliest known map of Honolulu in 1816. A detailed representation of both the harbor and the village, this chart accompanied the Russian-language edition of Kotzebue's narrative.

Occasional Papers of the Bernice P. Bishop Museum, vol. 24, no. 17, Aug. 1980, 315–333; Fitzpatrick (1986): 15–24, 46–64; Barrow (1978): 112, 160–161.

Meteorological Observations

The ancient Hawaiians had words for specific kinds of weather: *lā* for sunny, *ua* for rain, *'ino* for storm, *wela* or *hahana* for hot, and *anu* or *anuanu* for cold.

The earliest meteorological observations using instruments were recorded by Captain James Cook's men at Waimea Bay, Kaua'i.

On January 29, 1778, David Samwell's journal noted "light breezes & fine weather, the Therm[r] from 74° to 77°."

American missionaries, apparently near Kawaiahao Church, made the first systematic weather observations over an extended period. From August 1821 through July 1822, they reported an annual mean of 75 degrees, with a range from 61 to 88 degrees.

Dr. Charles Byde Rooke initiated rainfall records in Honolulu in 1837. He tracked monthly barometric pressures, temperatures, wind directions, and rainfall and published his meteorological observations in *The Hawaiian Spectator*.

The first official weather service under governmental auspices was established within the Hawaiian Government Survey in 1882, under Curtis J. Lyons. In 1890, Lyons assembled existing temperature records going back to 1821, as well as government data for 1883 to 1889, and published them in his first *Report of the Assistant in Charge of Meteorology*. In 1900, he initiated regular rainfall reports. Hailed as "the first accredited meteorologist of Hawaii," Lyons died in 1914 at eighty-one.

The U.S. Weather Bureau opened its Honolulu office in September 1904, with headquarters on the second floor of the Alexander Young Building and instruments on the roof of the building's makai tower.

Honolulu newspapers began to carry daily weather forecasts in 1903. On February 7, *The Advertiser* inserted a small box on its front page: "Weather Forecast for Today. Strong trades, possibly some rain." Discontinued after a year, the newspaper forecasts were resumed in 1921.

Weather satellites came into use during the 1960s. On April 1, 1960, the first pictures were received from Tiros I. Regular use of such satellites for Hawaiian weather forecasts began in 1965 and 1966.

Pukui and Elbert (1986); Beaglehole (1967): 1084; Ellis (1969): 22; *The Hawaiian Spectator*, Jan. 1838, 107, and succeeding issues; Curtis J. Lyons, *A History of the Hawaiian Government Survey* in Surveyor's Report for 1902 (1903): 18; Office of Government Survey, *Report of the Assistant in Charge of Meteorology* (1890); Curtis J. Lyons, *The Rainfall of the Hawaiian Islands* (Hawaiian Weather Bureau, 1902); HA, 20 Sept. 1922, 4, 7; F, Oct. 1914, 236–238; HAA 1906: 157–159; PCA, 1 Sept. 1904, 4, 9; PCA, 7 Feb. 1903, 1; PCA, 9 Jan. 1890, 3; HSB, 11 Feb. 1921, 1; HA, 28 May 1921, sec. 2, p. 1; HSB, 1 Apr. 1960, 1, 1A; HSB, 15 July 1965, B2; HA, 3 Mar. 1966, A1, A2.

Seismographs

In 1903, the U.S. Coast and Geodetic Survey installed a Milne seismograph at its Barbers Point Magnetic Observatory, the first such instrument to become operational in the Territory of Hawai'i.

The magnitudes of Hawaiian earthquakes, however, were not routinely determined locally until 1958. Before then, Island earthquakes were usually measured by mainland seismographs.

Furumoto, Nielsen, and Phillips (1972): 3, 7; F, Aug. 1899, 64.

Tide Gauges and Tables

Hawai'i's earliest tide gauge was installed near the entrance to Honolulu Harbor by the Hawaiian Government Survey in 1872. After just a few months, it quit working and no observations were made until a replacement gauge from the U.S. Coast and Geodetic Survey was installed in 1877. This gauge lasted eight years before failing, and finally, in July 1891, modern recording began by the Hawaiian Government Survey.

The earliest tide tables for Honolulu were published for 1895 by the Coast and Geodetic Survey as part of its tables for the Pacific Coast. Tide calendars for Island waters did not appear until some years after World War II, the most notable examples being those published by the Hawaiian Dredging Company.

HAA 1875: 31–32; HAA 1893: 9; HAA 1895: 7–10; HAA 1896: 7; information provided by Doak Cox of the Hawaii Institute of Geophysics, 3 Dec. 1990; information provided by Stan Melman of the Hawaii Maritime Center and DeSoto Brown of the Bishop Museum, 7 Dec. 1990.

Volcanic Activity

The recorded history of volcanic activity in the Hawaiian Islands began with the arrival of the Christian missionaries. In 1823, Reverend William Ellis visited Kīlauea Crater during a trip around the island of Hawai'i. He provided the first description of the crater and recorded information from Hawaiians about eruptions that had taken place in the past. One eruption was placed about 1790 and another about 1750. Ellis also talked to John Young, who recalled that the most recent Hualālai eruption occurred in 1800 or 1801.

Haleakalā and Mauna Loa were also active in the late eighteenth and early nineteenth centuries. Haleakalā erupted just above La Perouse Bay around 1790. The earliest recorded eruption of Mauna Loa took place in 1832. (See also *Seismographs*.)

Macdonald, Abbott, and Peterson (1983): 56–58, 60, 62; *SSB&A*, 10 Jan. 1993, A5.

Energy Sources

Electricity

O'ahu residents were introduced to man-made electricity on June 19, 1838, at a lecture presented by Dr. Gerrit P. Judd before the Sandwich Island Institute. After demonstrating a series of electrical experiments, he offered to shock a member of the audience. A volunteer finally approached and was given a moderate shock.

SIG, 23 June 1838.

Electric Utility Companies

The Islands' first private electric utility, the Hawaiian Electric Company, was organized as a partnership on May 7, 1891. In 1893, it was awarded a government franchise to provide private buildings in Honolulu with electricity.

*This building was erected in 1887 to house O'ahu's first electrical
generation plant. The photograph was taken sometime after 1927.* AH.

The company's first job was lighting the new store of Egan &
Gunn.

HJH (1980): 92.

Gas

Gas lighting came to Honolulu largely through the efforts of
Henry MacFarlane, proprietor of the Commercial Hotel. As early
as June 1858, he imported a portable gas apparatus from San Francisco, in hopes of lighting not only his hotel but other buildings in
the vicinity. His first public use of this equipment took place on
November 2, 1858.

"On Tuesday evening last," reported *The Polynesian*, "Mr. E.
Burgess opened his spacious billiard saloon at the Commercial Hotel,
which was well attended, no doubt the novelty of the room being
lit up with gas proving a great attraction. There are four burners,
two over each Billiard Table, and they filled the large room with a

most brilliant light. Mr. Macfarlane is deserving of great credit for his indefatigable exertions in being the first to introduce gas on this island."

Within a year, gas lighting was extended to other parts of Honolulu. The 1859 legislature authorized a charter for the Hono-lulu Gas Company to erect gas works and lay pipes in the streets and buildings of the city. On October 26, 1859, the company turned on the gas for the first time, lighting the Seaman's Bethel (a church), Odd Fellows Hall, newspaper offices, principal hotels, major inter-sections, and numerous private dwellings.

HJH (1980): 91.

Geothermal Power

The generation of electrical power from Kīlauea Volcano was considered as early as September 1881, when King Kalakaua and William Armstrong, his attorney-general, visited Thomas Edison in New York City and discussed the possibility with the inventor.

Interest in geothermal power resumed in the 1960s and 1970s. In 1961, the Hawaii Thermal Power Company drilled four shallow wells in the Kīlauea East Rift Zone, but the wells were not deep enough to be economically viable. In 1973, a National Science Foundation-sponsored geothermal research well at the Kīlauea sum-mit attained high temperatures. Three years later, the federally funded Hawaii Geothermal Project-Abbott (HGP-A) tapped 676-degree steam near Pohoiki, the world's hottest well.

SSB&A, 13 May 1990, A8, A9.

Ocean Thermal Energy

The world's first at-sea OTEC (ocean thermal energy conver-sion) plant was commissioned May 29, 1979, at the University of Hawai'i's Snug Harbor research facility. The OTEC system uses the difference in temperature between the surface of the ocean and the water below to generate electricity. Called Mini-OTEC, the barge unit was towed to Keahole Point, Hawai'i, where it successfully produced 50,000 watts of electricity.

HJH (1980): 92.

Oil Refineries

Built in 1950, the first oil refinery in Hawai'i—Pacific Refiners, Ltd.—produced asphalt, liquefied petroleum (bottled gas), and other products derived from the processing of crude oil. The company was sold in December 1955 to Standard Oil Company of California.

Automobile and aviation fuels were first manufactured in Hawai'i in January 1962, when the second phase of the huge Standard Oil Refinery at Barbers Point was completed. Both this refinery and the earlier plant in Iwilei used crude oil imported from Sumatra and other far-off Pacific areas.

HSB, 2 June 1949, 21; *HA*, 3 Feb. 1950, 11; *HA*, 2 Mar. 1952, Mag., 8–9; *HA*, 8 Dec. 1955, A12; *HSB*, 2 Nov. 1960, 1, 1A; *HSB*, 10 Sept. 1961, Home, 3; *HA*, 12 Jan. 1962, A1, A2.

Oil Spills

Over the years, Hawaiian waters have been the scene of numerous ship groundings, sinkings, and other marine disasters, and many of these disasters have produced oil spills of one kind or another. Such spills used to receive little or no attention in the press, which tended to concentrate on the more dramatic aspects of shipwrecks and rescues.

One of the earliest spills with recorded environmental consequences took place January 3, 1932, at Kalaupapa, Moloka'i. The Inter-Island Steam Navigation Company's 1,519-ton steel steamer *Kaala*, caught in rough seas and a strong northerly wind, broke her moorings and was driven on the rocks. One of the survivors, Ed Marques, later recalled, "The next morning we went out to look at the *Kaala* and we could see how the crude oil had spread out from the ship and killed all the fish."

Hawai'i's first large-scale oil spill occurred October 29, 1984, when a Navy oiler ran aground 1,500 feet from the Honolulu International Airport reef runway. Although 50,000 gallons of jet fuel spilled, the spill was contained and prevented from reaching shore.

The first spill to cause serious damage took place January 20, 1987, when a Sause Brothers barge spilled between 12,000 and 21,000 gallons of fuel oil into the Moloka'i Channel. Several beaches were closed, and seabirds and ocean life from Hanauma Bay to He'eia were affected. The cleanup required one month and cost more than $100,000.

HJH (1989): 150; Thomas (1985): 173–174; HA, 4 Mar. 1989, A1B; HA, 22 Jan. 1987, A3.

Solar Energy

Emmeluth & Company, Ltd., advertised solar water heaters as early as December 1900. Household solar water heaters, typically made of closely spaced copper tubes or galvanized iron pipes, were a common sight in Hawai'i during the early 1930s.

HJH (1980): 92; *HJH* (1987): 157.

Steam Engines

Steam power was introduced in 1853, first at Līhu'e Plantation and soon after at Koloa Plantation. The earliest use of steam power in Honolulu occurred the following year, at the machine shop and flour mill built by D. M. Weston.

HJH (1980): 90.

Windmills

The earliest windmills in Hawai'i date to at least 1837, when the French artist J. Masselot pictured two of them atop thatched huts in the background of his lithograph of Elisabeta Kinau returning from church.

John Cook, who arrived in Hawai'i in 1844, claimed that the first windmill in Honolulu was erected in the yard of William French, in the middle of what is now Alakea Street between Hotel and Beretania Streets.

By 1879, advertisements for windmills were appearing in Honolulu newspapers.

HJH (1980): 90; *HJH* (1982): 150.

Communication

Ballpoint Pens

Eight years after the pen was invented in Hungary and more than seven months after its 1945 appearance in mainland stores, the first ballpoint pen was offered for sale in Hawai'i. The Liberty House advertised the Kimberly "Californian" at $12.50 just before Father's Day in 1946.

HSB, 13 June 1946, 3; Robertson (1974): 22.

Interisland and Transpacific Communication

Several efforts to establish interisland telegraphic communication by submarine cable were initiated in the 1880s and 1890s. Two segments were actually laid—one connecting Pūko'o, Moloka'i, with Nāpili, Maui, in 1889, and the other connecting O'ahu and

Moloka'i in 1890—but neither was successful. The only cablegram sent and received was transmitted from the cable ship fourteen miles back to Koko Head on April 2, 1890.

Interisland radio telegraphy was initially tried at the end of the century. In 1899, Fred J. Cross and R. D. Silliman organized the Inter-Island Telegraph Company, Ltd., bringing in Marconi wireless experts and building stations at Kaimukī and on Moloka'i, Lāna'i, Maui, and Hawai'i.

This wireless station, built at He'eia, Windward O'ahu, in 1912, established the first commercial radio telegraph service between the Islands and the Mainland. AH.

A successful test of the system was conducted in June 1900, linking downtown Honolulu with the Kaimukī station. Batteries for operating the transmitter were held up in quarantine, so the operators used an automobile to furnish the necessary current. The message sent was the first to wing its way across the city by the new system and the first west of the Rocky Mountains to be sent by wireless telegraphy.

After numerous failures, the company finally succeeded in sending an interisland message in November 1900, connecting Kaimukī (by way of a kite flown at Wai'alae) with Lae o ka Lā'au on Moloka'i. Commercial service commenced March 2, 1901.

In December 1902, the end of a Commercial Pacific cable was drawn up on land near the present site of the War Memorial Natatorium in Waikīkī. The cable was put into operation on January 1, 1903, linking Hawai'i and the mainland with telegraphic service. The westward extension of this cable, connecting O'ahu with Midway, Guam, and the Philippines, was completed July 4, 1903.

During the summer of 1912, the Federal Telegraph Company, using a transmitter at He'eia, established the first commercial radio telegraph circuit to San Francisco. Originally restricted to press stories and similar uses, the new wireless was opened to the general public on September 3.

The Mutual Telephone Company inaugurated interisland radio telephone service on November 2, 1931. The seven-year-old son of George H. Vicars of Honolulu made the first call—to his grandfather, James Webster, on Hawai'i, to wish him a happy birthday. Mutual introduced radio telephone service with the mainland a few weeks later, on November 20, 1931. A submarine telephone cable connection with the mainland entered service October 8, 1957. Interisland and Transpacific Direct Distance dialing was initiated January 16, 1972. (See also *Telegraph.*)

HJH (1979): 111–113.

Magazines

The first quarterly review in the Pacific region was *The Hawaiian Spectator,* issued in Honolulu from January 1838 to October 1839.

HJH (1979): 109.

Mail

The earliest recorded piece of Hawaiian mail was a letter written by Sybil Bingham, a member of the first group of missionaries, from "Hanaloorah, Woahoo," on June 27, 1820, to Mrs. Fanny Howell of Canandaigua, New York. The letter was carried privately by ship to Boston, arriving on March 22, 1821, and then by regular mail to its destination. (See also *Postal Service.*)

Meyer (1948): 6.

Mail Chutes

A newspaper account of the opening of the four-story Judd Building at Fort and Merchant Streets (now the First Federal Savings and Loan Building) on March 15, 1899, noted that "a mail chute, the first in these Islands, forms one of the conveniences."

PCA, 16 Mar. 1899, 5.

Newspaper Advertisements

The earliest newspaper advertisements appeared in the first issue of Hawai'i's pioneer English-language paper, the *Sandwich Island Gazette and Journal of Commerce,* on July 30, 1836. The four-page weekly carried ads for clothing, hardware, household goods, ship chandlery, food, paper, saddles, a physician, a barber, and a mason.

Newspapers

The first newspaper published in Hawai'i was *Ka Lama Hawaii* (The Hawaiian luminary), a four-page Hawaiian-language weekly issued by the press of Lahainaluna Seminary from February 14 to December 26, 1834. Intended primarily for the students, it was edited by the Reverend Lorrin Andrews, illustrated with woodcuts, and printed in editions of two hundred copies each. A second Hawaiian-language newspaper, *Ke Kumu Hawaii* (The Hawaiian teacher), was printed semi-monthly at the mission press in Honolulu from November 1834 to May 1839.

Page from Ka Lama Hawaii ("The Hawaiian Luminary") for April 18, 1834, early in the 10-month run of the kingdom's first newspaper. HHS.

The *Sandwich Island Gazette and Journal of Commerce*, a four-page weekly, was the earliest English-language newspaper. It was published in Honolulu from July 1836 until July 1839.

Initially published on September 4, 1866, the first daily newspaper in the Islands, *The Daily Hawaiian Herald*, was suspended on December 21 of the same year.

The first daily newspaper with a Sunday edition, appearing June 17, 1900, was *The Honolulu Republican*.

HJH (1979): 109; HJH (1993): 242.

Postal Service

The second of the three "organic acts" of 1845 and 1846 provided for the establishment of a postal system, but four years elapsed before the law was implemented. Equally important was the treaty, signed December 20, 1849, providing for the exchange of mail between the United States and the Kingdom of Hawai'i. The first bag of mail received from San Francisco under this agreement arrived in Honolulu early in December 1850. The first eastbound bag under the same arrangement appears to have left Honolulu around November 7, 1850.

On December 20 of that year, the Privy Council issued a "Decree Establishing a Post Office in Honolulu," to be located in the office of *The Polynesian*, and named Henry M. Whitney, Esq., postmaster. (See also *Mail* and *Stamps*.)

Meyer (1948): 12–14.

Postmarks

The earliest postmark on mail from Hawai'i was a straight-line hand stamp reading "Honolulu, Hawaiian Is.," with a movable date. The oldest existing example of its use is dated November 7, 1850. (See also *Stamps*.)

Meyer (1948): 17.

Radar

Hawai'i received its first radar equipment around Thanksgiving in 1941, when the U.S. Army set up five mobile units at various locations around O'ahu. On December 7, at 7:02 A.M., the operators at 'Ōpana, the station near Kahuku Point, reported a large radar blip moving toward O'ahu. Their superior, assuming the men had picked up an incoming flight of B-17s, told them, "Well, don't worry about it." The blip, of course, was the Japanese attack force, and Oʻahu remained unaware of its approach until the bombs started falling.

Lord (1957): 44–48; Prange (1986): 372.

Radio Audience Surveys

Early in 1935, the Honolulu Chamber of Commerce distributed some 60,000 questionnaires in the Islands' first listeners' preference survey. Respondents numbered 5,618, of whom 5,369 owned radio receivers.

Sixty percent of the owners reported listening directly to mainland stations, an unsurprising finding since Hawaiʻi at that time had only two commercial outlets, KGU and KGMB. The most popular programming was "sweet dance music." The Jack Benny program, then the top-ranking show on the mainland, was only ranked eleventh in Hawaiʻi.

HSB, 13 Apr. 1935, 14; HJH (1987): 115–116.

Radios

Hawaiʻi's first radio broadcast took place in 1900. This pioneering effort, like most radio broadcasting during the first two decades of the century, involved telegraphic impulses rather than spoken words and music. (See *Interisland and Transpacific Communication.*)

The earliest broadcast of music and speech in the Territory occurred around October 1920 when M. A. Mulrony and T. C. Hall transmitted nearly an hour of talk and records from the Electric Shop in downtown Honolulu to the Pacific Heights home of their only known listeners, Tong Phong and his family. Such broadcasts from the Electric Shop became relatively frequent beginning in April 1921.

Also in 1921, Wah Chan Chock became Hawaiʻi's first licensed amateur ("ham") radio operator.

The first commercial broadcasts took place on May 11, 1922,

when both KGU, owned by *The Advertiser*, and KDYX, owned by the *Star-Bulletin*, went on the air. In what was described as a "hot race," both newspapers claimed victory. The first spoken words appear to have been a few "hellos" uttered by M. A. Mulrony into the KGU microphone and "distinctly heard by the Electric Shop" at 10:57 A.M. Fifteen minutes later, at 11:12 A.M., Governor Wallace Farrington inaugurated programming over KDYX with the greeting "aloha." This was followed by several talks and musical selections. The first scheduled program on KGU was a concert aired from 7:30 to 9:00 that evening. It began with a violin solo by Kathleen Parlow, "Ave Maria," and closed with selections by Johnny Noble's jazz orchestra.

Despite changes in ownership, studio location, frequency and power, KGU has survived to the present time, but the *Star-Bulletin* station discontinued operation in January 1924.

Automobile radio sets were first sold in the Islands in April 1930.

The direct transmission of mainland sports events to Hawai'i was first undertaken in the fall of 1930. On November 22, KGU experimentally broadcast the first quarter of the California-Stanford football game. Two weeks later, the station aired the entire Notre Dame-USC game from the Los Angeles Coliseum. Both accounts were carried by short wave to Honolulu, where they were immediately rebroadcast on the standard radio band. Previously, mainland games had been "re-created" by Honolulu announcers from telegraphically transmitted reports.

On Christmas morning 1930, KGMB originated a ten-minute segment of an international holiday program on NBC. The Honolulu portion was transmitted by short wave to California and then by wire to stations affiliated with the network. The event was hailed as the first time a Hawaiian program was transmitted to the mainland. Island radio stations began carrying mainland programs on a regular basis late in 1931.

On August 1, 1931, KGU presented its first weekly network series, *Split Second Tales*, transmitted from NBC on an experimental basis. Finally, on November 14, 1931, KGU became a "regularly authorized allied station" of the National Broadcasting Company.

Less than three months later, on February 8, 1932, KGMB affiliated with the Columbia Broadcasting System.

The first frequency modulation (FM) radio stations appeared in Hawai'i in 1953. KVOK, a low-power educational station, was licensed September 21, 1953, and survived until May 22, 1964. KAIM-FM, a commercial station specializing in religious and classical music broadcasts, received its license November 3, 1953. (See also *Interisland and Transpacific Communication.*)

HJH (1978): 106–108; *Polk-Husted Directory Co.'s Directory of Honolulu and the Territory of Hawaii* for 1920 (p. 1367), 1921 (p. 1439), and 1922 (p. 1489); HA, 3 May 1922, 9; HA, 9 May 1922, 9; HSB, 12 May 1922, 9–10.

Satellites

Launched October 5, 1957, the Soviet Union's Sputnik was the first satellite to pass near Hawai'i. Radio signals from Sputnik were picked up at several Island locations as the satellite sped overhead.

An early application of the new technology was in weather satellites, which photographed portions of the earth's surface and transmitted the results to receiving stations for processing and analysis. Tiros I, the first U.S. weather satellite to be put in orbit, was launched from Cape Canaveral in 1960 and monitored by a group of Island meteorologists and other scientists atop a windy bluff at Ka'ena Point, O'ahu. In 1964, when the first Nimbus weather satellite went into operation, clear satellite photographs of the Hawaiian Islands became available.

The Hawaiian Telephone Company provided communications services for many of the satellite launches of the 1960s and early 1970s.

Transpacific telephone calls, formerly made by radiotelephone or submarine cable, were now sometimes expedited by satellites. Telstar, AT&T's communications satellite, was used by Governor William F. Quinn in July 1962 for a telephone call that traveled from Honolulu to California by cable, then by radio relay to Maine, and via Telstar to London.

The videophone added pictures to sound. On May 18, 1971, Governor John A. Burns in Honolulu and Shinobu Ichikawa, vice president of Japan's Federation of Economic Organizations in Tokyo, completed the first international videophone call via satellite.

HJH (1979): 114–115.

Stamps

On June 18, 1851, the Privy Council issued a decree that authorized the postmaster to put out stamps of appropriate denominations. The first stamps issued under this decree were the two-, five-, and thirteen-cent "Missionaries" printed in the government printing office and put on sale October 1, 1851.

The earliest perforated Hawaiian stamps were a two-cent issue, in sheets of fifty, printed on the mainland and received in Honolulu in May or June 1864.

Meyer (1948): 18–19, 21, 97, 187–188.

Telegraph

On June 12, 1857, a marine telegraph was put into operation at Diamond Head. This device was actually a kind of semaphore designed to send visual (rather than electric) signals to the post office in downtown Honolulu when an approaching ship was sighted.

True telegraphy, involving the electric transmission of coded messages through wires, seems to have reached Honolulu some fifteen years later. On October 19, 1872, *The Advertiser* reported, "The Telegraph—The line connecting Mr. Rawson's store and Mr. Eckart's jewelry manufactory, is now in successful operation, and a crowd of the curious have been flattening their noses against Kinney's front window to see the machine work. For the sake of satisfying everybody, messages will be sent over the wires for a few days from 12:30 to 1 o'clock P.M., when anyone can witness their transmission."

The earliest commercial telegraph system in the Hawaiian

Islands was constructed in 1877 and 1878 on Maui. On September 1, 1877, *The Advertiser* printed a letter from its correspondent at Makawao, which stated: "Mr. C. H. Dickey has just completed a line of telegraph from his place at Haiku to his store in Makawao— a distance of about five miles. . . . Mr. Dickey has succeeded in making arrangements to continue the line to Wailuku, and it is sincerely hoped that there will be enough live men to be found there to run the wire over the mountain to Lahaina."

Soon thereafter, Dickey and his associate, C. H. Wallace, formed the Hawaiian Telegraph Company, with plans to connect Haʻikū, Makawao, Wailuku, Lahaina, and eventually Honolulu. The Haʻikū-Wailuku link was put into operation on February 21, 1878; the extension to Lahaina was operational five months later. (See *Interisland and Transpacific Communication*.)

HJH (1979): 109–110.

Telephone Directories

Hawaiʻi's first telephone book appeared in 1894, the same year in which Hawaiian Bell (founded in 1880) merged with Mutual Telephone Company (founded in 1883). The *Mutual Telephone Co. Official Directory, May, 1894* listed approximately 1,100 Oʻahu numbers.

This pioneering directory was, however, preceded by a broadside listing of numbers, dated July 1886.

The "Yellow Pages" came two decades later, when the *Telephone Directory, Honolulu, April 1914* included a "Classified Business List."

Simonds (1958): 24–25, 27; Forbes (1992b): 124.

Telephones

Like the first commercial telegraph, the earliest telephone in Hawaiʻi stemmed from the efforts of Charles H. Dickey on Maui.

Early telephones, probably dating from the 1880s. AH.

Years later, Dickey wrote, "In 1878, I received a letter from my brother, J. J. Dickey, superintendent of the Western Union Telegraph at Omaha, describing the new invention. . . . Before the year was out . . . I sent for instruments and converted my telegraph line into a telephone line."

On April 11, 1878, Dickey submitted his application for a caveat (a kind of provisional patent), asserting his "intention to introduce into the Hawaiian Islands the Invention known as The Bell Telephone."

The Maui telephone system was apparently put into operation in May or June 1878; a letter from Makawao, dated June 27, 1878, and printed in *The Advertiser*, boasted that "the telegraph and telephone are old here, 'everybody has 'em.'" The 1880–1881 directory, published in 1880, noted that the Hawaiian Telegraph Company "was established in 1877, and was the pioneer line of the Kingdom, and is up to the present time the only public line."

The telephone seems to have been introduced to Oʻahu soon after its appearance on Maui. In 1878, S. G. Wilder, minister of the interior, had a line installed between his government office and his lumberyard, and other private lines quickly followed. Organized service in Honolulu began during the fall of 1880, and on December 30, the Hawaiian Bell Telephone Company was incorporated.

Honolulu telephones were converted to dial operation in August 1910, but the last manual phones in Hawaiʻi (at Kamuela and Kapoho) were not phased out until 1957.

Annoyed by the growing numbers of freeloaders who used merchants' phones for their private calls, the Hawaiian Bell Telephone Company forbade free calls from stores and other public places and, in 1935, installed the first pay phones in Honolulu.

On May 5, 1986, Hawaiʻi's first official cellular telephone call was recorded. Glenn Umetsu, president of Honolulu Cellular Telephone Company, made a call to Hideto Kono, chairman of the Hawaii State Public Utilities Commission, from Tamarind Park in downtown Honolulu, using a $2,800 handheld unit. Commercial operation of cellular systems, both by Umetsu's firm and by GTE Mobilnet Hawaii, was scheduled for July.

HJH (1979): 110–111; HSB, 6 May 1986, A13.

Teletype

The teletype made its first appearance in Honolulu in 1929, but the service was too expensive for most users. In February 1945, however, *The Advertiser* announced the regular delivery by radio teletype of all United Press night-leased-wire news reports from the mainland.

In 1947 and 1948, the Mutual Telephone Company linked the major islands with a multi-channel, high-frequency radio delay system, which permitted the company to replace its radiotelegraph service (and operators) with radioteletype. Hawaiian Airlines immediately made use of this innovation, operating the first all-island radioteletype communication system.

Transpacific teletype service was greatly expanded upon the completion of the first submarine telephone cable between Hawai'i and California in 1957.

HJH (1979): 114.

Televisions

Television came to Hawai'i in late 1952. Station KGMB-TV was first, initiating regular programming at 5:05 P.M., December 1. "Hello, everybody," said Carl Hebenstreit into the camera as the first program, a twenty-five-minute assemblage of interviews, began. This live show was followed by a Gene Autry movie, a children's show (*Time for Beanie*), Hopalong Cassidy, and another movie (*Meet John Doe*). KONA-TV, which had telecast the first Island test patterns as early as November 17, began scheduled programming on December 16.

Television sets were advertised for sale six weeks before the start of actual programming. On October 16, 1952, Bergstram's announced, "TV is Nearer Than You Think!!! Buy a Quality TV Radio-Phonograph. Buy the magnificent Magnavox." Nine days later, Von Hamm-Young ran ads for Zenith sets.

Color television was first viewed in Hawai'i on May 5, 1957, when KHVH-TV presented a program of color slides and movies. Although only fifty O'ahu residents owned color sets at the time, the program was seen by many others in the Hawaiian Village Hotel lobby and the nearby aluminum dome auditorium.

Live television broadcasting to and from the mainland was inaugurated on November 19, 1966, when KHVH-TV used the Lani Bird communication satellite to bring the Michigan State-Notre Dame football game to Island viewers. At half-time, the station transmitted some Waikīkī scenes back to the mainland. The transmissions in both directions were in color.

The first cable television firm in Hawai'i was Kaiser-Teleprompter. It began service April 20, 1961.

HJH (1978): 108–109; HJH (1979): 113; HA, 16 Oct. 1952, sec. 3, p. 1; HSB, 25 Oct. 1952, 3.

Writing

Captain James Cook and his officers and men, writing in their journals, introduced the written word to Hawai'i in 1778. Their language was English, and their words were intended as personal records to be read primarily by other English-speaking persons.

The earliest written message intended for native eyes may have been the letter addressed by Simon Metcalfe, commander of the snow *Eleanora*, to the chiefs at Kealakekua, March 22, 1790, demanding the return of his boatswain, John Young, who was being detained ashore by Kamehameha. This is the oldest official document filed in the Archives of Hawai'i.

"The first correspondence in Hawaiian," according to Hiram Bingham, took place early in 1822. Kuakini "sent for the lessons we had printed in his language and was quickly master of them. But a few days passed before I received a letter from him, which I immediately answered in the Hawaiian, under date of Feb. 8th, 1822."

AH, Foreign Office and Executive File; Bingham (1849): 157.

Transportation

Airplanes and Air Service

J. C. "Bud" Mars made the first airplane flight in Hawai'i aboard a Curtiss P18 biplane on December 31, 1910. Mars made four flights from Moanalua Polo Field that afternoon, rising to an altitude of 500 feet the first time and 1,500 feet the last.

On June 10, 1911, Clarence H. Walker, piloting another Curtiss biplane, veered into a *hala* tree while landing at Hilo with a coughing engine—the first airplane crash in Island history.

Flying a biplane at Schofield Barracks on July 13, 1913, Tom Gunn took up airplane passengers for the first time—a local tailor and a young woman who was a ticket taker at the Empire Theater. The first paying passenger, Mrs. Newman of Honolulu, paid twenty-five dollars on October 2, 1913, for a fifteen-minute flight over Honolulu Harbor with Gunn.

The earliest interisland flight was made by Major Harold M.

Clark of the Fort Kamehameha Aero Squadron. He successfully flew to Moloka'i and back on March 15, 1918.

The first interisland airmail flight took place on July 3, 1919. Two Army seaplanes, commanded by Lieutenant Colonel B. H. Atkinson and Major J. B. Brooks, left Luke Field, Pearl Harbor, at 9:10 A.M. for Hilo with a bag of mail and reached the crescent city shortly after 1:00 P.M. without mishap. The return trip was made four days later.

In Hawai'i's first airplane fatality, Corporal Mark P. Grace of the Sixth Aero Squadron, Fort Kamehameha, was killed when his plane fell from a height of 3,500 feet as it failed to come out of a tail-spin maneuver. Amazingly, the pilot of the November 19, 1918, flight—Second Lieutenant Cary Crowdes—received only slight injuries.

Although simple landing strips were built at Schofield Barracks and elsewhere in the earliest years of Island flying, Hawai'i did not have a formally established airport until Luke Field on Ford Island was dedicated on April 29, 1919. John Rodgers Airport (later re-

Commander John Rodgers and his crew flew this Navy seaplane most of the distance from California to the Islands in 1925, but ran out of gas and had to finish the trip under sail and tow. AH.

named Honolulu International Airport) was built in part with funds appropriated by the 1925 territorial legislature and dedicated on March 21, 1927, thus becoming the first formally designated civilian airfield in Hawai'i.

The first flight between the mainland and Hawai'i took place in 1925. Flying a two-engine PN-9 Navy seaplane, Commander John Rodgers and a crew of four left San Pablo Bay (near San Francisco) August 31 and managed to reach a point 300 miles from Maui before running out of gas. With improvised sails, the plane floated the rest of the way, reaching Ahukini Harbor, Kaua'i, on September 10.

Lieutenant Lester J. Maitland and Lieutenant Albert F. Hegenberger flew a U.S. Army Fokker C-2-3 Wright 220 tri-motor, *Bird of Paradise,* from Oakland, California, to Wheeler Field on June 28 to 29, 1927. This was the first fully successful flight between the West Coast and Hawai'i.

The first complete crossing of the Pacific by air took place in 1928, when Charles Kingsford-Smith and his crew of three flew their Fokker tri-motor, *Southern Cross,* from California to Australia by way of Hawai'i and Fiji. They left Oakland Airport on May 31 and reached Wheeler Field on O'ahu the following morning. Following a short hop to Barking Sands, Kaua'i, they took off on June 3 for

The *Bird of Paradise* landed at Wheeler Field, completing the first successful Mainland-Hawai'i flight on June 29, 1927. *AH.*

Inter-Island Airways, Ltd., established in 1929 as the Territory's first full-scale interisland airline, flies one of its Sikorsky amphibians past Mānoa Valley. AH.

Suva and Brisbane and on June 10 ended their journey at Sydney. Six years later, Kingsford-Smith and Patrick Gordon Taylor repeated this crossing but in the opposite direction. Flying a single-engine Lockheed Altair, *Lady Southern Cross*, they left Brisbane in mid-October 1934 and, after stops at Suva and Honolulu, landed in Oakland on November 3. The last leg of this flight, from Wheeler Field to Oakland Airport, was the first eastbound flight between Hawai'i and the mainland.

The first interisland airline, Hawaiian Airways, Ltd., began operating November 9, 1929, and made more or less regular trips between the Islands as well as sightseeing tours. The firm suspended regular service in January 1930 and went out of business the following June.

The first full-scale local airline was Inter-Island Airways, Ltd. (now Hawaiian Airlines), which inaugurated scheduled operations on November 11, 1929, using two Sikorsky S-38-c seven-passenger amphibians and a Bellanca monoplane.

Inter-Island was awarded an airmail contract on September 20, 1934. Regular airmail service between the Islands began on October 8.

The first airmail flight linking the West Coast with Hawai'i occurred November 22 to 23, 1935, when a Pan American Airways Martin M-130 four-engine flying boat, *China Clipper*, flew from Alameda, California, to Pearl Harbor. The next day it continued westward to Midway, Wake, Guam, and Manila.

On October 21, 1936, Pan American initiated weekly passenger service between San Francisco and Manila via Honolulu. Seven passengers made the inaugural flight on the *Hawaii Clipper*, leaving Alameda at 3:11 P.M. and docking at Pearl City at 7:54 the following morning, October 22. The one-way fare between Honolulu and the West Coast amounted to $360.

The first jet aircraft flown in the Islands was a Lockheed TO-1 Shooting Star, piloted by Captain Paul Ramsey. For its maiden Hawai'i flight, the jet took off from Barbers Point Naval Air Station on October 26, 1948, and made a twenty-five-minute, 580-mile-per-hour dash to Honolulu and back. (A year earlier, in October 1947, the Navy had brought in a Ryan Fire-Ball, a hybrid powered by both piston and jet engines, but the Lockheed was the earliest true jet aircraft in Hawaiian skies.)

On December 13, 1955, a British Overseas Airways Corp. De Havilland Comet III jet airliner arrived at Honolulu International Airport on a goodwill flight around the world, thus making it the first civil airport in the nation to get a preview of commercial jet aircraft operation. The Comet remained in Honolulu for two days and gave a series of courtesy flights to government officials, aviation people, and tourists.

Commercial jet aircraft service was introduced to Hawai'i in 1959. Qantas Empire Airways began jet service on July 29, connecting Sydney, Nadi, Honolulu, and San Francisco with Boeing 707 aircraft. Pan American, the first domestic carrier to use jet airplanes on the Honolulu run, inaugurated 707 service between the West Coast and Tokyo via Honolulu and Wake on September 5. United Airlines began its DC-8 service to the Islands in March 1960.

Hawai'i saw its first SST (supersonic transport) on November 12, 1986, when a British Airways Concorde arrived at Honolulu International Airport. The 1,350-mile-per-hour jet aircraft had required only two hours and fifteen minutes to fly from Oakland, a new record. (See also *Balloon Flights.*)

HJH (1979): 105–107; HJH (1993): 241; HA, 13 Nov. 1986, A3.

Automobiles

The first automobiles appeared on the streets of Honolulu on October 8, 1899, the date on which both Henry P. Baldwin and Edward D. Tenney took possession of their newly arrived vehicles. *The Advertiser* reported the next day that "Hon. H. P. Baldwin's

Prince Kuhio and his wife were photographed sometime after September 1901 in this turn-of-the-century automobile, one of the earliest in the Islands. AH.

automobile, the first to be seen in the Hawaiian Islands, was given its first trial yesterday afternoon . . . [on] King street and out along Punahou street. . . ." The *Bulletin* noted that "E. D. Tenney's automobile, which with H. P. Baldwin's were the first to arrive in Honolulu, was tried for the first time Sunday afternoon by the owner. . . ." Both cars were described as Wood electrics.

City Transfer Company purchased a Reo in 1912, the first truck ever seen in Hawai'i. Its two-cylinder engine developed sixteen horsepower and permitted speeds up to twenty miles per hour.

On March 9, 1901, taxis (see *Taxicabs*) and U-drive motor cars were introduced by the Hawaiian Automobile Company. The company brought in approximately twenty-five electrics, for use either as hacks or self-driven vehicles. Their advertised range of twenty-five miles without recharging proved somewhat optimistic, and the automobiles were found to be very unreliable. The firm suspended operations on June 24, 1901, and in October a warehouse fire destroyed twenty-two of the cars in its fleet.

The first recorded motor vehicle death in Hawai'i occurred five years later, on June 4, 1906. Louis Marks and three passengers, descending an 'Aiea driveway in reverse, backed their car, a Winton, over a twenty-foot embankment. The vehicle made a complete somersault and fell on top of Marks, killing him instantly. Charles A. Bon was seriously injured, but both wives were thrown clear.

The Marks accident was only one of many reported in 1906, but none of the others appears to have had fatal consequences. At least six of the ninety motor cars on O'ahu were involved in major accidents that year.

Hawai'i's first automobile theft took place the evening of July 4, 1900. Spying Louis Grant's electric horseless carriage parked on Beretania Street near Fort, Pat Corcoran, a fireman who "had been celebrating the Fourth," jumped in and tried to start the motor. Unsuccessful in this effort, he then tried pushing the vehicle down the street, eventually leaping aboard and randomly moving the controls. When these maneuvers likewise failed to start the car, Corcoran contented himself by ringing its bell. A policeman who had witnessed these events gave chase and collared the would-be thief under the hose wagon in the fire station. "Judge Wilcox concluded that Corcoran had tried to elope with the auto and fined him $25 and costs," reported *The Advertiser*.

Driver's licenses were first issued in 1906. By May 14, forty-three applications had been received for chauffeur certificates, and sixteen of the applicants had been examined by "Chauffeur Expert" H. A. Wilder and had been awarded their licenses. The list began with the names of Dr. Herbert, Frank H. Tunison, C. M. Schoening, D. C. Kaimauoha, Gerritt P. Wilder, and Lloyd S. Schmidt. All forty-three were apparently males.

On Saturday afternoon, August 17, 1912, "the first real auto race meet ever held in Honolulu was successfully run off at Kapiolani Park," according to a *Star-Bulletin* account. The report observed that no accidents or fatalities occurred among the participants or spectators. The winning time in the five-mile event was 5:57, indicating an average speed of 50.4 miles per hour.

HJH (1979): 102–104; HSB, 19 Aug. 1912, 1, 7; HS, 14 May 1906, 8.

Balloon Flights

The first balloon flights in Hawai'i were unmanned. An entry in Andrew Bloxam's diary, written in Hilo on June 22, 1825, noted that the officers and men of the *Blonde* delighted a large native audience by setting off "some rockets, and a paper air balloon, but the latter caught fire almost immediately and falling on Lord Byron's grass house was near setting it in flames."

A more successful effort occurred late in 1840, while Hannah Holmes was entertaining sixty officers of the American exploring expedition then visiting Honolulu. She summoned her guests outside to watch the ascension of a balloon filled with hot air—perhaps the earliest record of such an event on O'ahu. In July 1858, Honolulu residents watched a number of illuminated balloons (one measuring twenty-eight feet in diameter) sent into the air from Henry MacFarlane's Commercial Hotel.

Manned balloon flights were first attempted in 1889 when Emil

Kapiolani Park Race Track

On Saturday, Nov. 2d,

At 3 o'clock p. m.,

Grand Sensational

Daring Attraction!

SCIENTIFIC AERIAL EXPLOITS!

The Prevailing European and American Sensation!

VAN TASSELL BROS.,

The Acknowledged Premier Aeronauts of the World.

The Heroes of over 200 Balloon Ascensions and Parachute Jumps.

They guarantee to ascend with their Monster Balloon to the dizzy height of one mile and jump to mother earth with only the support of their frail Patent Parachute.

Admission 50cts.; Children 25cts.

☞ Any failure of the above, all money will be refunded by Mr. L. J. Levey, who will handle the receipts.

☞ Tickets for sale at L. J. Levey's office. F. FROST.
102 Manager.

PREPARING TO JUMP.

Ad for Joseph Van Tassell's balloon ascent, the first successful manned ascent in Island history. Van Tassell tried to duplicate this feat November 18, 1889, but drifted out to sea and drowned.

L. Melville unsuccessfully tried to make a hot-air balloon ascension from Kapi'olani Park. A week later, he tried again in Iwilei. This time he was dragged through a *kiawe* thicket, carried about 300 yards at rooftop level, and finally forced to leap to the ground from a height of thirty feet.

On November 2, 1889, Joseph Lawrence Van Tassell took off from Kapi'olani Park, rose to an altitude of one mile, and then came to earth by parachute. On November 18, he tried to duplicate this feat in an ascent from Punchbowl, but the wind carried him off course, and he parachuted into Keʻehi Lagoon and drowned. Van Tassell appears to have been Hawaiʻi's first successful flyer, first parachutist, and first air fatality.

HJH (1979): 104–105.

Bicycles

The first bicycle in Hawaiʻi (called a "velocipede") arrived in January 1869. The first "safety" bicycle seen in the Islands, a Columbia, came in 1892.

HJH (1979): 102.

Bridges

Nobody knows when bridges were first constructed in Hawaiʻi, but published references date to 1825. Visiting Hilo on June 13 of that year, C. S. Stewart recorded the presence of a footbridge over the Wailuku River.

"A rude bridge crosses the stream just above the falls," he wrote later, "and it is a favorite amusement of the natives to plunge from it . . . into the rapids."

Although Nuʻuanu Stream, the northwestern boundary of early Honolulu, would seem to have been a prime candidate for bridging, the first bridge over it wasn't built until 1840. Located on Beretania Street, ʻEwa of Maunakea Street, it was the first major span in the Islands.

HJH (1986): 151–152.

Freeways

The first freeway constructed in Hawai'i was the Mauka Arterial, later called Lunalilo Freeway. The three 'Ewa-bound lanes of the six-lane divided highway, extending a distance of one mile between Old Wai'alae Road and Alexander Street, were opened to traffic November 9, 1953. The Kaimukī-bound lanes along the same stretch were opened and the highway was formally dedicated on January 5, 1954.

HJH (1979): 101–102.

Gliders

Hawai'i's pioneering glider ascent took place on Reservoir Avenue, Kaimukī, on October 23, 1910. Two brothers, twelve- and fourteen-year-old Malcolm and Elbert Tuttle, constructed the glider from plans published in the July 1910 issue of *Woman's Home Companion*. On the day they completed the craft, the boys carried it—fifteen feet long, eighteen feet wide, and forty pounds in weight—to the hillside site, where they launched it by running into the wind. On his third try, Malcolm rose ten feet in the air and traveled forty feet. Elbert photographed the event just before the glider was damaged by a gust of wind.

HJH (1990): 117–128; HSB, 8 May 1990, B1, B4.

Helicopters

Piloted by Captain Jack E. Beighle, the earliest helicopter flight in the Islands took place at the Hawaiian Air Depot, O'ahu, before August 3, 1945. The Sikorsky R-6A helicopter had been received in sections and was assembled by a Hawaiian Air Depot crew.

HSB, 3 Aug. 1945, 5.

Hydrofoils

Sea Flite made its first scheduled interisland passenger trip by hydrofoil on June 15, 1975. On its inaugural run, the *Kamehameha*, a ninety-two-foot, 191-passenger, forty-five-knot vessel, took 120 persons from Honolulu to Maʻalaea, Maui. In 1978, service by the three jetfoil vessels in the fleet was discontinued.

HJH (1979): 101.

Motorcycles

Motorcycles were apparently first brought to Hawaiʻi in February 1901. A 1902 introduction, however, has also been reported.

HJH (1979): 102.

Parking Meters

In August 1951, the Hawaii Aeronautics Commission installed the Islands' first parking meters in the parking lot at Honolulu International Airport. Each of the 101 meters required one cent for twelve minutes of parking or five cents for an hour.

The Honolulu central business district did not have on-street parking meters until February 1, 1952. The earliest public off-street parking facility operated by the City and County of Honolulu opened at Beretania and Smith Streets on December 19 of that year.

HJH (1979): 104.

Public Transit

Beginning in the spring of 1868, the Pioneer Omnibus Line's horse-pulled vehicle—Hawaiʻi's earliest public transit—served various parts of Honolulu.

Twenty years later, on December 28, 1888, Hawaiian Tram-

Hawaiian Tramways Company's mule-drawn cars, one of which is shown here on South King Street, introduced true public transit to Honolulu in 1888. AH.

Honolulu Rapid Transit & Land Co. began operating electric street cars in 1901. This car was photographed in 1911. AH.

ways, Ltd., started mule-car service with four open cars. The company was taken over by the Honolulu Rapid Transit & Land Company (HRT) in 1903.

The first electric streetcars, run by the Pacific Heights Electric Railway Company, Ltd., connected upper Nuʻuanu Avenue and Pacific Heights. Using two open-sided thirty-passenger cars (plus two freight/mail cars), this line functioned from November 1900 until 1904 or 1906. HRT provided citywide streetcar service from August 1901 to July 1941.

HRT inaugurated bus service in 1915, initially using locally built vehicles. ACF (American Car & Foundry) buses were acquired from the mainland in 1928. Trolley buses operated on a number of HRT routes from January 1938 to the spring of 1958.

HJH (1979): 102.

Railroads

The earliest railroad installation in Hawaiʻi appears to have been a track a couple hundred feet in length built in Honolulu in

The Kahului Rail Road Co. was Hawaiʻi's pioneering rail common carrier, beginning operation in 1879. This locomotive, photographed around 1910, was built in the 1880s. AH.

1857 to remove material dredged from the harbor. Another railway was erected on the pier at Kawaihae in 1858.

The Kahului & Wailuku Railroad began passenger service on Maui in 1879, thus initiating the first rail common carrier in the Islands. The earliest steam locomotives were operated by the Kahului Railroad and a short line at Hilo, the latter initially mentioned in January 1880. The Oahu Rail and Land Company provided railroad service on O'ahu from 1889 to 1947.

HJH (1979): 101.

Road over the Pali and around O'ahu

Initially a rough foot path, the road connecting Honolulu and Windward O'ahu by way of Nu'uanu Pali was gradually improved during the last two-thirds of the nineteenth century. The earliest recorded work on the route took place in 1837. In 1844 and 1845, the footpath was replaced by a horse road.

The first wagon to descend the Pali road on the windward side did so in 1861, and the first such trip up the road took place two years later. Major improvements, greatly reducing gradients and widening and smoothing the route, were undertaken in 1897 and 1898.

The first wagon road around O'ahu was completed in October 1869. This thoroughfare—sixteen to twenty-four feet wide and seventy-eight miles long—ran from Honolulu through the 'Ewa district and over the Schofield Saddle to Kahuku and then to Kāne'ohe, where it connected with the existing trail over the Nu'uanu Pali. Six years earlier, in 1863, W. A. Aldrich made the first complete carriage trip around O'ahu, which took four days.

Kuykendall (1953): 24–25; Scott (1968): 536–544; Greer (1966): 22.

Ships and Shipping

On January 20, 1778, at Waimea, Kaua'i, Hawaiians saw their first foreign ships—the *Resolution* and the *Discovery*—commanded by Captain James Cook and Captain Charles Clerke.

The first vessel of foreign design to be built in the Islands was the thirty-six-foot *Britannia*. Captain George Vancouver's carpenters designed and constructed the ship in February 1794 for Kamehameha's navy.

The Hudson's Bay Company's *Beaver*, a 101-foot, 109-ton vessel built in England in 1835, was the first steamer to visit the Ha-

The first foreign ship seen by the Hawaiians was the Resolution, *captained by James Cook, in 1778. This model of the vessel is displayed at the Greenwich Marine Museum. AH.*

The Beaver, *shown here at Victoria, B.C., was the first steamship ever seen by Islanders. It arrived at Honolulu Harbor in 1836 under sail because its paddle wheels had not yet been fitted, so Hawai'i residents had to wait another decade to see a ship actually steam into port.* AH.

waiian Islands. The *Beaver*—still lacking paddle-wheels—called at Honolulu en route to Fort Vancouver, in what is today Oregon, in 1836. The first vessel actually to steam into the harbor was the *Cormorant*, on May 22, 1846.

Scheduled interisland service began in November 1846 when the 116-ton schooner *Kamehameha III* advertised twice-weekly sailings between Honolulu and Lahaina. She offered to carry mail, freight, and passengers. In 1849, however, the *Kamehameha III* was taken by the French and never returned.

The first interisland steamer voyage was a roundtrip between Honolulu and Lahaina. It was completed by the twin-screw *Constitution* on February 2, 1852.

Late in 1853, the Hawaiian Steam Navigation Company inaugurated the first scheduled interisland steamer service, using a 106-foot, 114-ton sidewheeler renamed *Akamai*. Frequently laid up, the *Akamai* was retired permanently in April 1857. The company was subsequently reorganized, and on June 28, 1860, its new 399-ton screw steamer *Kilauea* arrived in Honolulu. Thereafter, steam navigation on this run operated on a relatively regular basis.

The Regular Dispatch Line introduced scheduled sailing packet service between Hawai'i and the mainland in 1855. Nine years later, it was joined by the Hawaiian Packet Line. Between the two lines, six fast-sailing vessels provided cargo and limited passenger services.

The California Steam Navigation Company began a regular trans-Pacific passenger and cargo service with the steamer *Ajax*, which arrived in Honolulu on January 27, 1866. After two unprofitable voyages, however, the operators gave up. A permanent scheduled steamer service connecting San Francisco and Honolulu was finally inaugurated by the California, Oregon, and Mexico Steamship Company, with the Honolulu docking of its SS *Idaho* on September 17, 1867.

Containerized cargo shipments began in August 1958 when several C-3 freighters were altered to carry containers on deck. In 1960, the *Hawaiian Citizen*, with a capacity for 436 twenty-four-foot containers, became the first all-container carrier in the Pacific.

Honolulu saw its first nuclear-powered merchant ship on December 22, 1962, when the NS *Savannah*, the world's first ship of its type, sailed past Aloha Tower and docked at Pier 39. This was more than three years after a nuclear-powered submarine (see *Submarines*) had first been stationed at Pearl Harbor.

HJH (1979): 99–101; HJH (1987): 156; Thomas (1985): 27–29, 212; SSB&A, 23 Dec. 1962, A1.

Shipwrecks

Long before the beginning of Hawai'i's written history in 1778, Hawaiian canoes—some quite large—were presumably lost at sea, driven against reefs and rocks, and otherwise disabled. Almost nothing is known today of such pre-contact disasters.

When Thomas G. Thrum initiated his long-running chronology of marine casualties in 1882, his earliest entry was the legendary wreck of a foreign vessel, *Konaliloa*, at Ke'ei, on the south side of

Kealakekua Bay. Thrum dated this event around 1620, although others think it may have occurred a century earlier. Both the captain and his sister struggled ashore and were taken in by the natives.

In the spring of 1796, Kamehameha sent a fleet of war canoes to invade Kaua'i. Nearing the island, many were swamped by high winds and rough seas. The survivors returned to O'ahu.

The first recorded loss of a Western vessel occurred later that year, on October 31. The British brig *Arthur*, commanded by Captain Henry Barber, struck a coral shoal off Laeloa (now Barbers Point), O'ahu, and was driven onto the rocks. Six of the twenty-two men aboard were killed.

The first steamship lost in Island waters was the *West Point* in 1856. Leaving Koloa, Kaua'i, with a cargo of oranges, the *West Point* steamed into a strong squall and was swept back onto the rocks and destroyed.

HAA 1882: 31–35; Dibble (1909): 19; Gibbs (1977): 17, 26–29, 33–34, 76, 84; Kuykendall (1938): 47–48.

Space Travel

Several astronauts made their first landfalls in Hawai'i after splashing down in the Pacific Ocean. Walter M. Schirra circled the earth six times in the Sigma 7 spacecraft before dropping into the water 1,300 miles northwest of Hawai'i. He was picked up by the carrier *Kearsarge* and then flown to Hickam Air Force Base for a three-hour layover on October 6, 1962. About 1,000 Islanders greeted him.

On July 26, 1969, the first men on the moon, Neil A. Armstrong, Edwin E. Aldrin, Jr., and Michael Collins, arrived at Pearl Harbor aboard the carrier *Hornet*, which had picked them up after the splashdown of their Apollo 11 craft, *Columbia 3*.

The first Hawai'i-born astronaut, Major Ellison Onizuka, made his initial flight into space aboard the shuttle *Discovery*, January 24–27, 1985. A year later, on January 28, 1986, Onizuka died in the explosion of the space shuttle *Challenger*, soon after takeoff from Cape Canaveral, Florida.

HJH (1979): 107; HA, 28 Jan. 1985, 1; *Time*, 10 Feb. 1986, 24–31; Ogawa and Grant (1986).

Submarines

The first submarines permanently homeported in Hawai'i were the U.S. Navy's *F-1* and *F-3*, which arrived under tow on August 1, 1914, and the *F-2* and *F-4*, which arrived on August 24.

The first submarine disaster in American naval history occurred on March 25, 1915, when the *F-4* sank in 306 feet of water off Honolulu Harbor, with the loss of all twenty-one officers and men on board.

The first nuclear-powered submarine to be homeported at Pearl Harbor was the *Swordfish* (SSN 579). It was stationed there early in 1959 and deactivated November 19, 1987.

HJH (1979): 101; information from Commander Submarine Force, U.S. Pacific Fleet, Public Affairs Office, 4 Mar. 1988.

The first submarines permanently homeported in Hawai'i arrived in August 1914. They lined up for this dockside photograph early the following year. AH.

Taxicabs

"For the first time in the history of motordom in Hawaii," stated the *Star-Bulletin* on January 24, 1914, "taxicabs have come to Honolulu, and seven cars, all of the Ford variety and of the enclosed type, started work this noon under the auspices of the Honolulu Taxicab Company."

Five additional Model T's were expected. The cabs were unmetered, relying instead on flat rates. The minimum charge, applying to a short (under one mile) city trip, was fifteen cents per passenger. A trip from downtown Honolulu to the Moana Hotel for either one or two passengers was seventy-five cents. A tour around the island came to $17.50.

An earlier taxicab venture, in 1901 (see *Automobiles*), was unsuccessful.

HSB, 24 Jan. 1914, 5, 8.

Traffic Laws

Territorial legislatures were quick to recognize the arrival of the motor car. Act 54 of the 1903 session imposed an annual tax of five dollars on all vehicles "drawn by horses or mules, and automobiles used for the conveyance of persons." Act 27, passed in 1905, required "every automobile, bicycle, tricycle or vehicle" to keep lights burning "when in use during the hours of darkness." The same legislature set a four-mile-per-hour automobile speed limit over bridges and increased the annual tax to twenty dollars. Two years later, the legislators provided for stiff fines, ranging from five dollars to $500, for "furious or heedless driving." In 1911, they began requiring a "metallic tag" with year and registration number, to cost the owner an additional twenty-five cents.

The first comprehensive "Traffic Ordinance" (as it was officially named) was passed by the Honolulu Board of Supervisors and approved April 7, 1914. This ordinance established the "Congested Traffic District," between Richards Street and Nu'uanu Stream makai of Beretania Street. Fort Street between Queen and Beretania and Hotel and King Streets from River to Alakea Streets were further designated a "Special Traffic District." An ordinance approved June 13, 1914, imposed a thirty-minute parking limit between 8 A.M. and 10 P.M. in the Special Traffic District. At the time this law was enacted, only 1,782 motor vehicles were registered on Oʻahu.

The Honolulu Board of Supervisors first mandated street signs posting parking restrictions, speed limits, and other traffic controls in 1920.

SLH 1903, Act 54; SLH 1905, Acts 27, 60, 89; SLH 1907, Act 68; SLH 1911, Act 146; HHR, Jan. 1968, 426–432; RLH 1905, sec. 628, 629, 631; *Ordinances of the County of Oahu and City and County of Honolulu, T.H., July 1, 1905 to Jan. 4, 1915*: Ord. No. 56 and 64; Schmitt (1977): 430–432; Ord. No. 176, in *Rev. Ord., City and County of Honolulu, 1923*, sec. 445.

Traffic Lights

The first traffic lights in the Islands were installed at the intersection of Nuʻuanu Avenue and Beretania Street in Honolulu in 1936. The overhead signal was put into operation on February 19.

HJH (1979): 104.

Tunnels

The first tunnel constructed on a public highway in Hawaiʻi was built on the Olowalu-Pali section of the Lahaina-Wailuku Road. Completed on October 10, 1951, the tunnel was 286 feet long, thirty-two feet wide, and more than twenty-two feet high.

HJH (1979): 101.

Buildings and Amenities

Air Conditioning

Hawai'i's earliest recorded experiment with air conditioning took place at the Hawaiian Opera House, at King and Mililani Streets, in 1912 or 1913. Electric fans were placed behind large tubs filled with blocks of ice to blow cool air toward the audience.

W. A. Ramsay, Ltd., agent for the Carrier Corp., had the first fully air-conditioned offices in the Islands. This novelty was announced in a half-page newspaper advertisement in September 1935.

Later that year, Ramsay provided air conditioning to the Hawaii Theater. In 1936, the Cooke Trust Company offices, the new Waikiki Theater, and the Queen's Hospital asthma ward also received air conditioning.

The first store with air conditioning was probably McInerny's shop on Merchant Street, which had the equipment installed in 1926 or 1927. The first fully air-conditioned home was built in 1938.

Honolulu Dept. of Housing and Community Development, *Housing and Community Development Research*, No. 37, July 1977, 29–30, 34; *Building Industry Digest*, ASHRAE Supp., June 1985, 29–34.

Architects

John Young and Isaac Davis, two English sailors marooned on Hawai'i in 1790, built the first foreign-style masonry buildings, and thus may be considered the first architects in the Islands.

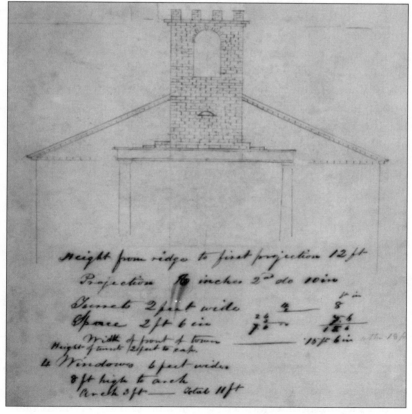

One of Hiram Bingham's architectural drawings for Kawaiahao Church. HHS.

Theodore C. Heuck, the first professional architect in Honolulu, arrived from Germany in 1850 and eventually designed the Queen's Hospital, the Royal Mausoleum, and Iolani Barracks.

The earliest known Hawaiian architectural drawings are Hiram Bingham's plans for Kawaiahao Church, dating from circa 1820–1842.

72nd Annual Report, HHS, 1963: 8, 10–11; Forbes (1992b): 71.

Astronomical Observatories

Hawai'i's first astronomical observatory, the College of Hawaii Observatory, opened on Ocean View Drive in Kaimukī on April 8, 1910. Built largely in response to the approach of Halley's Comet, the facility contained a six-inch telescope. The structure was still in use in 1929, although it showed obvious signs of deterioration. Termite-ridden and beyond repair, it was razed in 1958.

By the time of its demise, the Kaimukī observatory was already being replaced by facilities on the neighbor islands. The first of these was the Mees Solar Observatory at the summit of Haleakalā, completed in 1956. Thirteen years later, in 1969, the first of a series of world-class instruments was put into operation at the top of the state's highest mountain, Mauna Kea.

HJH (1976): 71; HA, 1 Apr. 1929, 4; HSB, 6 May 1958, 16; SHDB 1973: 203; SHDB 1987: 479.

Bathhouses

Three types of public bathhouses evolved in nineteenth-century Hawai'i, each serving a specific locale and clientele.

The earliest to appear—the downtown bathhouse—catered to hotel guests, sailors, and residents. Somewhat later, beachside bathhouses provided dressing rooms and showers for swimmers and sunbathers. Finally, toward the end of the century, the influx of Japanese laborers led to the development of community baths on many plantations.

Bathhouses like this one, photographed in 1860, were a common sight in Honolulu at least as early as 1840. AH.

Downtown bathhouses were in operation at least as early as 1840 when a list of Honolulu businesses included a "bathing house."

The Hawaiian Hotel featured both a bathhouse and a toilet structure on its grounds when it opened in 1872. A newspaper account reported that "on the grounds is a separate bath house, where guests can enjoy the luxury of hot or cold baths free of charge."

The 1904 city directory listed six public baths in Honolulu.

HJH (1982): 156–159.

Bathrooms

References to home bathrooms began to appear before the middle of the nineteenth century, although without any mention of their contents or exact functions. An 1846 advertisement, for example, described a house "sent from the U. States in frame . . . Bath rooms, Ironing rooms, Cook House, &c attached."

Beginning in 1850, Henry MacFarlane's Commercial Hotel

boasted its "Hot, Cold, and Shower Baths." The charge for a hot bath was one dollar; for cold and shower baths, the charge was fifty cents.

In 1859, the Sailor's Home advertised "Shower Baths on the Premises," and in 1861, the National House reported "Bath Rooms" and "Water Closets" on its property.

HJH (1982): 151–152, 155–156.

Bathtubs

By the middle of the nineteenth century, bathtubs were relatively common in Honolulu. Advertisements for basins, chamber pots, wash bowls, and wooden tubs appeared in 1838 issues of the *Sandwich Island Gazette*.

By 1847, newspaper ads specifically listed bathtubs for sale. Not until 1866, however, did an ad carry an illustration of the product in question. The one-column notice included a small cut of a woman seated in a high-backed tub.

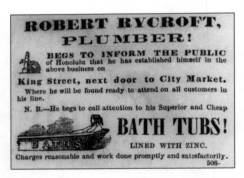

Bathing at this time often took place in backyard structures detached from the main dwellings. In 1863, Mary Allen gave this description of the tub behind her house along Nu'uanu Stream: "Out in the garden there was a small house built over a good-sized cement cistern and equipped with a platform and seats. Fresh, cool water from the stream flowed in one side and out the other, giving the bather a delightful cold water dousing."

Bathtub advertisement published in the Pacific Commercial Advertiser, February 17, 1866.

HJH (1982): 152.

Buildings

As early as 1809, a brick building served as Kamehameha's residence while in Lahaina. Built by "foreigners," possibly as early as 1800, it was the first Hawaiian palace built of permanent materials.

In 1854, *The Polynesian* reported that "a fine new Fire-Proof Store . . . built of brick, with a granite front, is something new in Honolulu." This structure, the Makee & Anthon Building at the corner of Ka'ahumanu and Queen Streets, was sent from Boston.

The first Honolulu structure built largely of concrete was the Kamehameha V Post Office at Merchant and Bethel Streets, which opened in March 1871.

Building permits were first required in 1886. The law covered all construction between Kalihi Stream and Mānoa or Kālia Streams, as well as churches, schools, hotels, and other public buildings elsewhere in the Kingdom. It excluded buildings costing less than $1,000.

Erected in 1854, the Makee & Anthon Building at Ka'ahumanu and Queen Streets was Honolulu's earliest office building, and the first described as fireproof. AH.

The Kamehameha V Post Office at Merchant and Bethel Streets, opened in 1871, was the first building constructed mostly of concrete. AH.

High-rise construction was unknown in Hawai'i before about 1900. Except for church spires, buildings were limited to two or three stories. The first four-story building was the Judd Block (now the First Federal Building), opened in March 1899.

Honolulu's first "skyscraper" was the Stangenwald Building at

The Judd Building, opened in 1899, was the earliest to reach four stories (a fifth was later added). At the far left, the neighboring Stangenwald Building was completed two years after the Judd Block and became the first building with six stories. AH.

119 Merchant Street. Completed in April 1901, this six-story office building was eventually surpassed by the Aloha Tower (ten stories, 184 feet, completed in 1926), Tripler Army Hospital (fourteen stories, 189 feet, completed in 1948), and many more recent buildings.

HJH (1981): 100–101.

Cemeteries

Early European visitors found a variety of burial practices in use among the Hawaiians. Ali'i were often entombed in *heiau* like the Hale o Keawe at Hōnaunau, built before 1700, or beginning around 1825, in the royal crypt on the Iolani Palace grounds. The bodies of commoners were deposited in caves or in shallow graves near the beach.

The first foreigner known to have died in the Islands was William Watman, a member of Captain James Cook's gunnery crew, who was killed by a paralytic stroke in January 1779 at Hōnaunau. At the request of the chiefs, he was buried ashore in the *heiau*.

The oldest cemetery headstone in Hawai'i, which originally marked the grave of Captain Charles Derby (died 1802) in the old graveyard for foreigners, near the present intersection of South King and Piikoi Streets. The headstone, carved in Massachusetts and erected around 1803, was eventually relocated to the small cemetery behind Kawaiahao Church, but Derby's remains could not be found. Schmitt photo.

A small cemetery for foreigners was established in Honolulu (apparently near today's King and Pi'ikoi Streets) as early as 1802. Both Captain Charles Derby, who died in 1802, and Isaac Davis, who died in 1810, were buried there. The cemetery was vacated around 1900.

The Hawaiians soon began to adopt Western burial practices. In 1822, Mrs. Maria Loomis wrote, "Today a funeral procession was formed, and the corpse of the young man who died yesterday was carried past our house, and decently interred in the burying ground. This is the first instance of natives burying their dead after the manner of civilized nations."

Sometimes described as the "first public cemetery," O'ahu Cemetery opened in Nu'uanu in 1845. Two year later, *The Polynesian* listed four graveyards in use in Honolulu.

Oliver G. Traphagen designed Hawai'i's first crematorium, located at the rear of Nu'uanu Cemetery, in 1905. The building was completed in early 1907.

The first pet cemetery in the Islands was Valley Pet Memorial Park, located alongside Kahekili Highway near the entrance to the Valley of the Temples Memorial Park. The cemetery was consecrated in late 1975, and the first burial took place in February 1976.

Hiroa (1957): 565–580; *The Sales Builder*, Mar. 1940, 3–15; Beaglehole (1967): part 1, p. 516–517; Ii (1983): 83, 85, 87; Journal of Mrs. Maria Sartwell Loomis, Oct. 21, 1819, through May 25, 1824 (HMCS Library), entry for 11 Jan. 1822; *Hawaiian Spectator*, April 1838, 86; *32nd Annual Report, HHS,* 1923: 58–59; Cleveland (1842), I: 232; *Papers of the HHS*, no. 16 (1929): 6–7; PCA, 6 Feb. 1921, 2; HA, 21 July 1926, ed. p. [p. 12]; HA, 27 Feb. 1928, ed. p. [p. 12]; HJH (1967): 55; P, 9 Jan. 1847, 138; PBN, 12 Sept. 1977, 13; *Hawaii Architect*, Dec. 1980, 17; HAA 1907: 164–165.

Cooperative and Condominium Housing

Owner-occupied apartment housing, first in the form of cooperative units and later of condominiums, appeared on the market in the 1950s.

Although at least four large cooperative projects were announced between 1953 and 1955, none of these advanced beyond the planning stage. The first cooperative actually built, Diamond

The Waikiki Ambassador, 2957 Kalākaua Ave., became the State's first cooperative apartment structure in 1956. Schmitt photo.

Head Ambassador Apartments at 2957 Kalākaua Avenue, was completed in the summer of 1956. Prices for the one-bedroom units started at $12,750.

The Horizontal Property Regimes Act, passed by the 1961 legislature, was the first condominium law enacted by any state.

The first condominium project to receive state approval,

This building at 3019 Kalākaua Ave. was completed in 1961 to become Hawaiʻi's first condominium. Schmitt photo.

in 1961, was a twelve-story apartment structure at 3019 Kalākaua Avenue, near the base of Diamond Head. This building was already three-fourths complete when the developers decided to convert it into a condominium.

The first commercial condominium in Hawai'i was the 100 Wells-Kona, a single-story, 5,000-square-foot office building in Wailuku, Maui. Erected in 1961, it gained condominium status in March 1963, about the same time that work began on the first mainland commercial condominium.

HJH (1981): 105–106.

Dumb Waiters

The Hawaiian Hotel, erected on Hotel Street in 1871 and 1872, had a dumb waiter connecting the kitchen in the basement with the dining room above. No earlier recorded example has been found.

HAA 1877: 29.

Electric-Eye Doors

The first door equipped with an "electric-eye" mechanism to open automatically when approached was installed at the entrance to the Cooke Trust Company on Fort Street on May 22, 1939.

HSB, 22 May 1939, 3.

Electric Lights

Hawai'i's first experience with electric lights was in April 1879, when the English ironclad *Triumph* visited Honolulu. All ten of the vessel's twelve-ton guns and some of its lights were operated by electricity. After nightfall, the warship unexpectedly switched on its spotlight and for nearly two hours bathed the city in its beam.

The earliest use of electric lights ashore in Hawai'i appears to have been in Mill Number One of the Spreckelsville Plantation on Maui on August 21, 1881. To satisfy the curiosity of people anxious to see the "concentrated daylight," Captain Coit Hobron ran a special train from Kahului, and King Kalakaua, Dowager Queen Emma, and Princess Ruth were among those who came to view the lights.

Electric lights were first seen ashore in Honolulu on the evening of July 21, 1886, when the palace grounds, Palace Square, and Richards Street were illuminated by five arc lights as part of an exhibition arranged by C. O. Berger, a local businessman. Arc lights were similarly used at the king's jubilee birthday ball at the palace on November 25, 1886. By the end of April 1887, the palace had been wired, and the electrical generating machinery had been installed.

In March 1888, permanent electric street lights were turned on, and in November 1889, the government electric plant first provided power for the incandescent lighting of offices, stores, and residences. The earliest Christmas street lights were installed along Fort Street in downtown Honolulu on December 4, 1937.

Myatt (1991): 128; *HJH* (1993): 240; *HJH* (1980): 91–92; *SSB&A*, 23 Dec. 1990, A3.

Elevators

The first elevators in Honolulu appear to have been installed in the early 1880s, sometime between the issuance of the 1879 and 1885 fire insurance atlases. None is indicated on the 1879 map, but two elevators appear on the 1885 map—one in the Beaver Block at Fort and Queen Streets and the other in a general merchandise store at 16 Nu'uanu Avenue. Six elevators are shown in an 1886 supplement to the 1885 map, while forty-eight can be found on the 1899 map.

The first newspaper reference to an elevator in Hawai'i appeared in July 1882: "The handsomest building that has lately been erected here is undoubtedly Mesrs. (sic) Wilder & Co.'s store and office. . . . The elevator, a powerful machine, is opposite the freight door."

The earliest electric elevators were in the Emmeluth Building, on King Street at Bishop, and the Mott-Smith Building (later The Hub), at Fort and Hotel. Both were three-story brick structures completed in 1897.

HJH (1981): 102–103.

Escalators

The first escalator in the Islands was installed in the House of Mitsukoshi, a department store at King and Bethel Streets, in December 1940. The escalator was limited to upward traffic between the first and second floors.

The first two-way escalators were placed in operation in 1947, when Sears Roebuck and Company opened the second floor of its Beretania Street department store.

HJH (1981): 103.

Fire Escapes

The Boston Block on Fort Street, completed in 1900, had Honolulu's first external fire escapes.

Hawaii Architect, Dec. 1980, 16.

Fire Hydrants

In 1852, five fire hydrants were placed along Nu'uanu Avenue, and cisterns were constructed at various street intersections. The hydrants served to prevent a recurrence of the fiasco that took place a few years earlier when Honolulu's first firefighters mistook a cesspool for a well. (See also *Fire Departments* under GOVERNMENT AND SOCIAL SERVICES and *Water Supply*.)

HJH (1980): 99; HJH (1982): 151.

Fire Sprinklers

In September 1920, the Hawaiian Pineapple Company, Ltd., in Iwilei was the first company to install automatic fire sprinklers.

HJH (1980): 99.

Forts

Hawai'i's first forts—one in Honolulu and the other at Waimea, Kaua'i—were erected by Dr. Georg Schaeffer's Russians in 1816. The Honolulu fort was begun as a blockhouse trading post at the foot of what is now Fort Street and completed as a full-scale fort by Kamehameha after he had evicted the would-be Russian colonists. It was finally dismantled in 1857. Fort Elizabeth on Kaua'i was razed in 1865.

W. F. Judd (1975): 41, 46, 98–99, 103.

The Honolulu Fort at the foot of Fort Street served as a military post, jail, and mental hospital from 1816 to 1857. AH.

Fountains

Hawai'i's first public fountains had a utilitarian purpose. They provided drinking water as well as a contribution to municipal art.

In 1867, the Temperance Legion erected an ornamental drinking fountain at the corner of King and Bethel Streets, on the grounds of the Seaman's Bethel Church, in the hopes that passing sailors might stop for a drink of water instead of patronizing the local grog shops. Designed and built for $300, this fountain ran continuously and relied on water offered free of charge by the government.

Three years later, a more ornate fountain was built near the entrance to the Court House. According to an item in *The Advertiser*, "At the corner facing Queen Street, will be an iron drinking fountain, not a constantly running one like that at the Bethel Corner, but worked by touching a spring, when the water issues forth, and stops when the pressure is removed."

In the early 1890s, a "playing fountain" was added to the grounds of the Hawaiian Hotel. This was one of the earliest fountains to have a purely decorative purpose.

F, 1 June 1867, 45; Scott (1968): 155; PCA, 5 Mar. 1870, 3; *Pacific Coast Commercial Record* (San Francisco), 1 May 1892, 5.

Geodesic Domes

In January 1957, Henry J. Kaiser erected one of the world's first aluminum geodesic domes as an auditorium for his Hawaiian Village Hotel in Waikīkī. Inexpensive and quickly assembled, the dome could accommodate 1,800 people.

HJH (1981): 108.

Hotels

Hawai'i's first accommodation for visitors was established sometime after 1810, when Don Francisco de Paula Marin opened his

The Volcano House was a pioneering tourist hotel overlooking Kīlauea Caldera on the Big Island. Photographed in 1866. AH.

home on the Honolulu waterfront on a commercial basis. Arranged around the Marin home were grass houses for the workers and guest houses for the ship captains who boarded with him while their vessels were in port.

Joe Navarro and Anthony Allen operated other early hostelries. Around 1820, Navarro's Inn stood on the mauka side of what is now Merchant Street. In 1823, Allen kept a boarding house for

Hawaiʻi's earliest major hostelry was the Hawaiian (later Royal Hawaiian) Hotel, erected in 1871–1872 at Hotel and Richards Streets. AH.

Waikīkī's first large resort hotel, the Moana Hotel, was opened in 1901 and considerably expanded in 1917. AH.

seamen and a small farm two miles from the Mission House, in Pawa'a.

The first hotel of any size—the Warren House—was opened by William K. Warren on Hotel Street near Bethel around 1825. Not only did it boast Honolulu's first good dining room, but it was also the earliest inn to feature musical entertainment for its guests.

The first hotels in Waikīkī were Herbert's in 1884, the Park Beach Hotel in 1888, and Waikiki Villa in 1889. (The Hotel Waititi was actually in Pawa'a.) The Moana Hotel, opened in 1901, was Hawai'i's first large resort hotel.

HJH (1980): 82–83; *HJH* (1993): 240–241.

Lighthouses

The earliest lighthouse in Hawai'i was built at Keawa'iki, Lahaina, and put into operation on November 4, 1840. Other early lighthouses were constructed at Kawaihae in 1859, again at Keawa'iki in 1866, and on Kaholaloa Reef at the entrance to Honolulu Harbor in 1869.

Dean (1991): 1, 2, 8–9, 61, 113.

Neon Signs

Neon signs first appeared in Hawai'i during the late 1920s. Opened in February 1929, the Gump's Waikiki shop on Kalākaua Avenue at Lewers Road had the first sign.

The first mention of neon signs in the city directory occurred in an Electric Supply Company advertisement in the 1929–1930 edition.

HJH (1980): 92.

Prefabricated Housing

Prefabricated wood-frame dwellings were relatively common in Honolulu during the first half of the nineteenth century. What may have been the earliest to reach the Islands was brought by the Russian frigate Neva from Sitka, Alaska, in January 1809. Acquired by Kamehameha, it was set up the following year by carpenters from the royal navy yard.

HJH (1971): 24–38.

Public Housing

The first public housing in Hawai'i (other than military projects) was Kamehameha Homes, built by the Hawaii Housing

Kamehameha Homes, opened in Kalihi in 1940, pioneered public housing. AH.

Authority at 1629 Haka Drive, Kalihi. It was occupied on July 19, 1940.

HJH (1981): 103–104.

Residential Subdivisions

The earliest residential subdivision activity occurred under government auspices in the 1840s. On November 14, 1846, the Home Office inserted an ad in *The Polynesian*: "The Minister of the Interior is prepared to sell or lease Building Lots between Honolulu and Waikiki, on application being made according to law."

In 1849, Theophilus Metcalf drafted a plat map for Kulaokahu'a (bounded by today's Alapa'i Street, Kīna'u Street, Makiki Stream, and King Street), showing newly assigned street names and lot lines. Except for initial interest in the parcels fronting on Thomas Square, however, sales and development in this tract remained slow for many years.

HJH (1993): 241–242.

Sewers

Construction of a sewer system for Honolulu began in August 1899. By mid-1901, almost thirty-four miles of sewers had been completed.

Even at the outset, many urban areas remained unserved, and over the next half century, the system could not keep up with the rapid growth of metropolitan Honolulu.

Substantial extensions of the original system were made in 1907 and in the 1920s. As late as 1929, only 75 percent of the dwellings in Honolulu and 40.3 percent of all dwellings on O'ahu were connected with street sewers, and privy vaults and cesspools were still deemed to be serious problems.

HJH (1982): 160–162.

Sidewalks

Hawai'i saw its first sidewalk in 1838, its first brick sidewalk in 1857, and its first concrete sidewalk in 1886.

The Advertiser was so taken with the concrete sidewalk that in March 1886 it advised its readers to "examine the sidewalk in front of Mr. Waterhouse's store [on Queen Street] and see for themselves" the handiwork of "Mr. John Bowler, the well-known plasterer."

HJH (1979): 101; PCA, 26 Mar. 1886, 3.

Street Pavement

Fort Street was macadamized from the waterfront to Kukui Street early in 1881, thus becoming the first paved thoroughfare in Hawaii.

On February 12, 1881, *The Advertiser* commented, "The construction of well-macadamized road-ways in its principal streets ought to mitigate one of the summer plagues of this city."

HJH (1979): 101.

Time and Timepieces

The first timepieces seen by the Islanders were those on Captain James Cook's ships or carried by their officers. These included two "Watch Machines," an "Astronomical Clock," an "Alarum Do.," and a "Pinchback pocket Watch." The watch-machine, or marine chronometer, was an extremely accurate and sophisticated timepiece, essential for determining longitude.

Hawaiian royalty, ali'i, and early haole settlers apparently possessed timepieces at an early date. For example, in 1812, King Kamehameha's return for a shipload of sandalwood included a large clock.

The earliest newspaper advertisements for watches appeared in 1840, when Henry Paty & Company placed announcements in both the *Sandwich Island Mirror* and *The Polynesian*.

Large public clocks emerged in the 1840s and 1850s. In 1842, James Hunnewell presented Kawaiahao Church with a large church clock. The earliest "tower clock" in Hawai'i was an 1825 instrument removed from an older church in Valparaiso, Chile, and installed around 1846 in the Cathedral of Our Lady of Peace, where it still resides.

Throughout most of the nineteenth century, Islanders observed local time, which differed for every meridian crossing the archipelago. In Honolulu, for example, midnight by Greenwich time occurred at 1:28:33 P.M. (marked by a blast from the Lucas Planing Mill whistle). Hilo time ran eleven minutes and twenty seconds ahead of Honolulu time; Waimea, on the west side of Kaua'i, lagged Honolulu by seven minutes and thirty-six seconds.

Hawai'i finally adopted standard time on January 13, 1896, when all public timepieces were set in accordance with "Hawaiian Standard Time," which was ten hours and thirty minutes behind Greenwich time.

In 1947, the territorial legislature advanced Hawaiian Standard Time by thirty minutes, making it ten hours (instead of ten and a half) slower than Greenwich time, effective the second Sunday of June.

The Islands briefly tried daylight-saving time on several occasions, beginning in 1918, but were finally exempted from it by the 1967 legislature.

HJH (1992): 207–225.

Toilets

Already common, although far from universal, in both Europe and the eastern United States, the flush toilet was apparently unknown in Hawai'i in the mid-nineteenth century.

Its first confirmed use was in King Kamehameha IV's new house on the Iolani Palace grounds in 1856. Expenditures for the project in 1856 and 1857 included "water traps for closets," "digging cesspools," "oil casks for cesspool," "plumbers bill," and "fixing water closets."

Washington Place, built between 1844 and 1847 and now thought to be the oldest continuously occupied residence in the Islands, was one of the earliest private dwellings to have modern plumbing. Formerly the home of Queen Liliuokalani and now the residence of Hawai'i's governor, Washington Place had a bathroom next to the queen's bedroom, probably installed in the latter half of the nineteenth century.

Newspaper advertisements began addressing flush toilets later in the century, noting in 1879, "Water pipes! . . . House Plumbing Materials, such as Earth Closets, . . . Hose Bibb Cocks, Sewer and Sink Traps, Urinals. . . " for sale. By the 1890s, J. Emmeluth & Company offered the new porcelain water closets at both their stores, aimed at making slophoppers and outhouses obsolete.

HJH (1982): 152–153.

Wallpaper

In 1819, the first wallpaper reached Hawai'i. It was installed in the Marshall and Wilder two-story frame house, a prefabricated structure built on the Honolulu waterfront.

HJH (1971): 25–26.

Water Supply

Water supply and sanitation were relatively primitive in the early days of Honolulu. The residents commonly relied on water from springs and streams, sometimes carrying calabashes of water great distances over rugged terrain. Sewers did not exist.

Work on a piped supply system for Honolulu was first undertaken in 1847 and 1848. The completed line conveyed water from a taro patch mauka of Beretania Street to a water tank erected in the basement of the new Harbor Master and Pilots' Office, near the wharf at the foot of Nu'uanu Avenue.

By 1851, a small masonry reservoir had been completed near Nu'uanu Avenue and Bates Street. It was connected to the harbor by a four-inch iron main and served the vessels coming into port as well as the businesses and dwellings along its route.

Honolulu's system was sporadically extended and improved, but it remained inadequate well into the twentieth century.

As late as the 1920s, homes in the uplands did not receive a regular supply of water, and others only received unfiltered, muddy water from Nu'uanu. No substantial progress on solving these problems was achieved until the creation of the Board of Water Supply in 1929.

HJH (1982): 149–151.

Wells

On June 27, 1820, Maria Loomis visited "a Black man native of Schenectady named [Anthony] Allen" who drew his water "out of an excellent well and I believe the only one on the Island."

Four months later, Loomis recorded that Captain Daniel Chamberlain "has completed digging a well, and found good water in a bed of coral seven or eight feet below the surface of the earth. This, with the exception of Mr. Allen's of Witete [today's Pawa'a], is the first ever completed on this Island."

Another early well digger was Joseph Navarro, who dug a well in his yard near Bethel and King Streets in 1822.

The first artesian well in the Islands was drilled in the summer of 1879 near James Campbell's ranch house in 'Ewa.

HJH (1981): 106; HJH (1982): 150; HJH (1987): 157.

Wharves

Hawai'i's earliest known wharf for accommodating large visiting ships was built around 1825 at Honolulu Harbor, a little north of the foot of Nu'uanu Street. It consisted of a sunken hulk that had been hauled in and placed there. In 1837, the hulk was removed and a substantial wharf was built in its place.

HAA 1891: 143.

Currency and Banking

Banks

The first bank represented in Hawai'i was Page, Bacon & Company of San Francisco and St. Louis. As early as June 1854, a Honolulu merchant served as an agent for this bank; a separate branch operated from November 1854 until December 1855.

The first permanent bank, Bishop & Company, opened on August 17, 1858, as a partnership between Charles R. Bishop and W. A. Aldrich. The bank accepted sums up to $300 and paid 8-percent interest if the funds were left deposited for three months. Bishop & Company changed names several times over the years and is currently known as First Hawaiian Bank.

HJH (1980): 84; Joesting (1983): 31–33; Tilton (1927): 56.

Billionaires

Hawai'i's first resident billionaire was Barbara Cox Anthony, a Cox Newspapers heiress whose assets were estimated at $1.1 billion in *Forbes* magazine's 1986 list of the 400 wealthiest Americans. Anthony ranked fifteenth on the national list, sharing the spot and a $2.2 billion fortune with her sister, Anne Cox Chambers of Atlanta.

HSB, 13 Oct. 1986, A1.

Credit Cards

Hawai'i's first credit cards were offered by oil companies during the 1920s, but the concept of credit did not become popular until after World War II. By 1958, the Credit Bureau of Hawaii estimated that 75 percent of all Honolulu businesses issued their own cards.

On October 1, 1958, the American Express Company's credit card plan, serving a large number of participating merchants, went into effect in the Islands. In January 1959, the Diners Club credit system was begun with only nineteen participating firms and 2,000 cardholders. Seven months later, it served more than 200 businesses and 10,000 cardholders in Hawai'i.

The earliest local credit card plans, the Bank of Hawaii's Charge Account Plan and the Kamaaina Charge Club, also began operations in 1959.

HSB, 24 Sept. 1958, 49; HSB, 20 Aug. 1959, 21; SSB&A, 3 Apr. 1960, Home sec., 5.

Credit Unions

The first Island credit union to receive a federal charter was the Big Island Educational Credit Union in Hilo. Chartered in August 1936 as the Big Island Teachers Credit Union, it began operations on September 24 of that year.

HJH (1980): 84. Another source gives the charter date as April 27, 1936; see HJH (1988): 230–233.

Industrial Loan Companies

Industrial loan companies in Hawai'i can trace their origins, in part, to the *tanomoshi* formed by Japanese immigrants working at Island plantations in the late nineteenth century. A more direct ancestor was HAX Finance Ltd., initiated in 1933 as the financing arm of Hawaiian Auto Exchange, a used-car firm. Enactment of the Territorial Industrial Loan law in 1937 led to the creation of numerous additional companies.

SSB&A, 16 Jan. 1977, A1, A5.

Money

The first paper money engraved in Hawai'i was printed at Lahainaluna Seminary in 1843. Intended for use inside the school, it consisted of heavy squares in denominations ranging from three cents to one dollar.

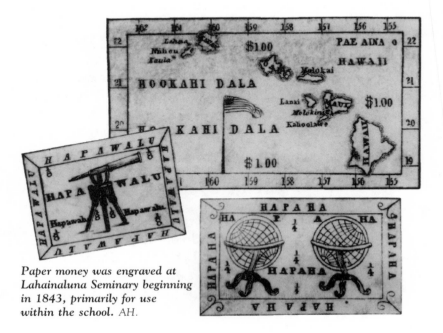

Paper money was engraved at Lahainaluna Seminary beginning in 1843, primarily for use within the school. AH.

Some of the earliest official paper currency was issued around 1880. AH.

These coins were the first issued for amounts greater than one cent, and were initially circulated in 1883. A copper cent had been minted in 1847. AH.

A copper cent, minted in 1847, was the first official coin of the Hawaiian Kingdom. It bore the likeness of Kamehameha III.

The first official paper currency consisted of certificates of deposit authorized in 1859 and issued in 1866 or 1867. In 1883, these silver certificates came in denominations of ten, twenty, fifty, and 100 dollars.

Coinage for amounts greater than one cent was authorized by the legislature in 1880. The first installment, $130,000 in silver half-dollar pieces, arrived in Honolulu on December 9, 1883; the first of these coins to go into circulation was received at the box office of the Music Hall the following evening.

Day and Loomis (1973): 26–27; HJH (1968): 96; HJH (1980): 100.

Savings and Loan Associations

The first savings and loan association in Hawai'i—and the only one in the United States to obtain its charter from a monarchy—was the Pioneer Building & Loan Association of Hawaii, chartered on June 12, 1890. Today, it is known as the Pioneer Federal Savings Bank.

HJH (1980): 84.

Stockbrokers

On November 15, 1879, William O. Smith & Company ran a one-column advertisement stating that "the undersigned have opened an office on Ka'ahumanu Street, Honolulu, for the purchase and sale of sugar and other Corporation Stocks, Bonds, and other similar securities, solely on commission."

Four years later, in 1883, a group of Island residents met and voted to establish a Honolulu Stock and Bond Exchange, but it was short-lived.

A more successful effort was made in 1898 when members of the new Honolulu Stock Exchange met and elected their first officers. This exchange survived until December 30, 1977, when it, too, was discontinued.

HJH (1980): 84.

Commerce

Advertising Agencies

Four "advertising agents" were listed in the 1900–1901 Honolulu directory's classified business section. All located downtown, they included the Pioneer Advertising Company under C. L. Clement, manager, and three smaller organizations operated by Robert Atkinson, Frank Godfrey, and Percival Russell.

Husted's Directory of Honolulu and Hawaiian Territory [1900–1901] (Sacramento: News Publishing Co., n.d.): 709.

Aloha Shirts

Aloha shirts were first sold in the mid-1930s. At that time, many local boys were wearing aloha-type shirts made of Japanese challis. Tourists seeing these shirts special-ordered them from local tailors, until Ellery J. Chun, who owned King-Smith Clothiers, decided to manufacture some of the shirts and keep them stocked in his store. His first shirt designs were hand-painted by his sister, Ethel Chun Lum. Ellery Chun registered "Aloha" sportswear in 1936.

Newspaper advertisements for aloha shirts first appeared in 1935. Some of the earliest were run by Musa-Shiya Shoten, Ltd., on North King Street near River. On August 2, 1935, for example, its ad proclaimed, "'Aloha' Shirts—well tailored, beautiful designs and radiant colors. Ready-made or made to order . . . 95¢ and up."

The new style eventually won wide acceptance. *Paradise of the Pacific* magazine published its first photograph of a man wearing an aloha shirt in 1938. Soon after, movie stars took up the fad. By 1940, officials of the territorial and city and county governments were allowing their employees to wear aloha shirts, at least in warm weather.

HJH (1980): 86–87; HA, 6 Oct. 1987, B1, B2; Steele (1984).

Barbers

William Johnson operated Hawai'i's earliest recorded barber shop around 1836 at some unspecified location in Honolulu. Johnson's ad in the early issues of the *Sandwich Island Gazette* proclaimed a "Shrine of Adonis! ! . . . Cuts, curls, and shaves, with taste and care."

SIG, 30 July 1836, 4; SIG, 6 Aug. 1836, 3; PP, Aug. 1940, 31.

Bars

Drinking places were some of the earliest retail businesses established in the Islands. Although both Hawaiians and foreign residents had been drinking hard liquor—either bought from visiting ships or distilled locally—for many years, no mention of bars or saloons occurs in the historical record until 1822. In April of that year, several "dram-shops" were observed in Honolulu. By November, Honolulu had seventeen grog shops operated by foreigners.

Identifying Hawai'i's first gay bar is far more difficult and probably impossible. Homosexuality (ho'okāmaka, ho'omāhū, moe) was known in ancient Hawai'i long before bars and saloons, straight or otherwise, first appeared. Grog shops and coffee houses patronized by homosexuals, either natives or sailors, may have existed.

Newspaper references to gay bars first appeared in 1963, but four more years elapsed before any were identified by name—The Apartment (at The Clouds), The Glade, and Yappy's Cocktail Lounge, among others.

Hawai'i's first topless nightclub was the Dunes on Nimitz Highway. In November 1964, Jack Cione, owner of the Dunes, initiated luncheon fashion shows featuring models and shoeshine girls who wore very little above the waist.

On January 4, 1973, Cione's Dunes unveiled its first topless and bottomless waiters and waitresses (the latter with shoes). Approximately 350 persons, most of them women, were on hand for the initial Thursday lunch. The naked waiters were said to be a world first.

HJH (1980): 80–81; Malo (1951): 65, 67; Handy and Pukui (1972): 73; Pukui and Elbert (1986): 220, 249, 459; Daws (1968): 164–168; Whipple (1973): 180–203; HA, 12 Feb. 1963, A1, A4; HSB, 29 Feb. 1964, 13; SSB&A, 24 Sept. 1967, A1, A1A; HA, 25 Sept. 1967, A1; HA, 26 Sept. 1967, B1.

Billboards

Large outdoor advertising signs first appeared in Honolulu during the last third of the nineteenth century and, judging from old photographs, grew rapidly in both size and number. As early as 1871, five- or six-foot-high posters promoting coming attractions were pictured lining the high fence in front of the Royal Hawaiian Theatre at Hotel and Alakea Streets. By 1897, full-size free-standing billboards advertising bars, plays, and especially tobacco products stood at a number of downtown locations. A few years later, these signs were appearing at Ward Street, McCully, and other outlying areas.

This proliferation of outdoor advertising encountered increasing public hostility. In 1905, for example, members of the Woman's Christian Temperance Union urged a boycott of "eatables" advertised on "those horrid posters and billboards." The Outdoor Circle, organized in 1912 to promote the island's natural beauty, decided in its first year to focus on the anti-billboard fight.

At first the campaign met with resistance or indifference, but the Outdoor Circle persevered and, in 1926, achieved victory. In that year, they bought out the last Honolulu firm handling outdoor advertising, tore down all remaining billboards on O'ahu, and secured a "gentleman's agreement" with major companies that promised to abide by the spirit of the Circle's campaign.

In 1927, the territorial legislature passed an act limiting billboards on O'ahu to the Honolulu central business district and setting their maximum height at ten feet, six inches. In 1961, Maui became the first neighbor island county to adopt a billboard control ordinance.

Scott (1968): 148, 190, 285, 289, 296, 331, 332, 437; *HS*, 3 Aug. 1905, 8; *PP*, Feb. 1948, 6–9, 32; *PCA*, 20 Sept. 1905, 9; *PP*, Nov. 1906, 8; *SLH* 1927, Act 195; *SLH* 1961, Act 88; *HSB*, 21 Oct. 1961, 1.

Bookstores

Books were initially sold in general merchandise stores or distributed by church-affiliated groups. By 1869, however, the first Honolulu city directory listed two full-scale bookstores. C. C. Bennett operated one store and offered stationery, books, and newspapers. Henry M. Whitney's store advertised foreign and domestic books, periodicals, and stationery.

F, 15 June 1846, 95; *F*, 19 Oct. 1852, 64; Bennett (1869): viii, xxvii.

Bottles

Hawai'i lacked a bottle-manufacturing plant in the nineteenth century, and all glassware needed by Island brewers, soft drink makers, and other bottlers had to be shipped in. Hawai'i's first embossed bottles were the soda bottles imported by Ulrich Alting, a German merchant, in 1851. Embossed whiskey bottles followed about seven years later.

Elliott and Gould (1988): 1, 6, 74, 116, 178; *Hawaii*, Feb. 1988, 59–60.

Business Registration

The Hawaiian government first registered corporations in the middle of the nineteenth century. Initially, only eleemosynary corporations were granted charters, beginning with Punahou School on June 6, 1849, and Kaneohe Church on November 19, 1849. The earliest business corporation approved by the minister of the interior was the Hawaiian Flour Company, in April 1856. The first partnership to be registered was Castle and Cooke, "general merchants and commission," filed by S. N. Castle and J. B. Atherton in 1880. The earliest registration of a trademark—covering Buhac insect powder—was on October 25, 1888, by Benson, Smith & Company.

HJH (1980): 85; *HJH* (1993): 240.

Celluloid

Although the date of celluloid's first appearance in Hawai'i remains unknown, this early plastic was certainly present by May 21, 1889, when Hollister & Company began to advertise Eastman Kodak cameras. These cameras, of course, used the new Kodak rollfilm, which was manufactured on a celluloid base. Later that year, Thrum's Up-Town Book and Stationery Store advertised "Celluloid Goods," and Popular Millinery House listed such wares as "Toilet cases in Celluloid, at $1.75 per box and upward." Such ads became quite common in the 1890s.

HG, 21 May 1889, 9; *PCA*, 17 Dec. 1889, 2; *PCA*, 24 Dec. 1889, 3.

City Directories

Chauncy C. Bennett compiled and published Honolulu's first directory in 1869. As part of this work, Bennett found it necessary to assign street numbers—Honolulu's earliest. Bennett's numbers lasted, more or less intact, for about a decade.

Bennett (1869); Greer (1966): 34–35; Forbes (1992b): 90.

Conventions

The earliest convention involving a written agenda, delegates, and published proceedings, appears to have been the 1823 General Meeting of the Sandwich Islands Mission, held at the Mission House on King Street on February 28. Three delegates met, formally founded the organization, and elected a fourth to membership. The handwritten financial report presented at the meeting reported the purchase of "5 galls wine, $15," "2 do Rum, $4," and "2 do Brandy, $6"—items presumably consumed during the course of a year, and not all at a post-session happy hour.

Similar general meetings of the Sandwich Island Mission took place at more or less regular intervals for many years, each session bigger than its predecessor. The 1848 session, held at the native school house in Honolulu, attracted thirty-seven delegates.

During the 1920s and 1930s, Hawai'i hosted many major conferences with international scope. The first of these was the Pan-Pacific Scientific Congress, during which 103 delegates from eight nations, plus forty observers from Hawai'i, convened at Iolani Palace and other locations, August 2–20, 1920. Some 138 papers were read at the scientific sessions. Many social events were also held.

HJH (1994): 109–111.

Dairies

In May 1823, missionary Charles S. Stewart noted that Anthony Allen kept a large herd of goats, whose milk supplied many of the captains in port as well as commercial agents.

The first commercial dairy, Puunui Dairy, was established in 1869 in Nuʻuanu Valley. No known bottles from the dairy still exist, but a delivery receipt reads, "September 30, 1875, Akong Proprietor." The dairy sold its milk for six cents a quart.

Since 1884, about 600 different dairies have been in operation in the Islands.

HJH (1992): 69; HHN, Sept. 1988, 3–5.

Department Stores

The 1916 edition of the Honolulu city directory was the first to include a category for "department stores." Only one was listed: B. F. Ehlers & Company, at 1026–1038 Fort Street. The Ehlers establishment, with origins dating to 1850, had previously been classified as a dry goods and apparel store. In 1918, B. F. Ehlers & Company became the Liberty House.

By 1947, the city directory listed sixteen department stores in the Territory. Only two—presumably the Liberty House and Sears—qualified to be so designated under the definitions of the 1948 U.S. Census of Business.

Polk-Husted Directory Co.'s Directory of Honolulu and the Territory of Hawaii 1916: 1203; Polk's Directory of City and County of Honolulu 1941–42: 420; Polk's Directory of City and County of Honolulu 1947–48: 578, 685, 1174; SHDB 1984: 680.

Electric Shavers

The electric shaver's earliest published mention in Hawaiʻi occurred in an advertisement by Hollister Drug Company on December 6, 1934: "Schick Electric Shavers/Finest Made/$15."

In 1934, the average daily earnings of unskilled male employees on the sugar plantations were only $1.63, so few Island men could
afford the luxury of an electric razor.

HSB, 6 Dec. 1934, 2; Schmitt (1977): 360.

Firearms

Captain James Cook and his men brought the first firearms to
Hawai'i when they landed at Waimea, Kaua'i, in January 1778. The
Hawaiians were quickly acquainted with the power of these guns.
Before the ships anchored, Captain Cook sent a party ahead in small
boats to discover an appropriate landing place. A Hawaiian who
came out to meet the boats attempted to grab a boat hook and was
shot and killed.

The Hawaiians hoped to acquire some of Cook's arms, but the
only guns he left behind were those taken from his body and from
his slain marines. However, the Islanders did not have to wait long
for additional weapons. Several early traders sold guns to Hawaiian
chiefs and encouraged the different factions to fight each other.

Kuykendall (1938): 14; Daws (1968): 32, 34–37.

Fish Canning

The MacFarlane Tuna Canning Company opened a plant in
Kewalo, Honolulu, and made its first export shipment to the coast
in May 1917. Several earlier efforts had been made to can ahi and
aku, apparently without success.

PCA, 25 May 1917, 7; HAA 1918: 169.

Furniture Stores

Charles Williams opened the first furniture store in Hawai'i in
July 1859 in Honolulu. A Massachusetts cabinetmaker who settled

in Honolulu in 1857, Williams offered cabinets, imported furniture, and wooden coffins at his store. Imported furniture was previously available only through sporadic shipments by local merchants.

Jenkins (1983): 141.

Grocery Stores

In the summer of 1855, Samuel Savidge and Henry May established the first real grocery store in Hawai'i. Initially located on King Street near the Seaman's Bethel, the store was shifted in subsequent years to Fort Street and finally to Beretania at Pensacola. It was later renamed H. May & Company and then May's Market before closing in January 1956.

The Kaimuki Super-Market, which opened in September 1938 at the corner of Wai'alae and Koko Head Avenues, was the first Island food store to be named a "supermarket." Unlike its postwar competitors, it offered delivery service and apparently lacked some of the features that characterize today's stores.

Hawai'i's first modern supermarket appears to have been the Manoa-Woodlawn Super Market at 2928 East Mānoa Road, Honolulu. Plans announced on March 24, 1946, called for a $65,000 market and drug store in a 6,000-square foot building, a service station, and parking for seventy-five automobiles, all occupying a one-acre site immediately makai of the East Mānoa bridge. This pioneering effort was followed by the Kapi'olani Super Market, opened at 1015 Kapi'olani Boulevard, Honolulu, on October 27, 1947, and announced by advertisements boasting of its self-service, central checkout system, and 16,000 square feet of parking.

HJH (1980): 81–82; HJH (1987): 157.

Holoku and Muumuu

The first holoku was made in 1820 for the high chiefess Kalakua by missionary wives aboard the brig *Thaddeus*. The holoku has been defined as "a loose, seamed dress with a yoke and usually with a train, patterned after the Mother Hubbards of the missionaries."

The muumuu is more difficult to date, but apparently evolved not long after the holoku. A loose gown, it omitted the yoke and sometimes had short sleeves.

Elizabeth Eberly, "The Story of the Holoku and the Muumuu" (Hawaii State Library System, pamphlet, 1973); *HA*, 14 May 1990, B1; Pukui and Elbert (1986): 78, 256.

Industrial Areas and Parks

Areas devoted primarily to industrial uses date to the early 1800s, when the Honolulu waterfront became the location of numerous shipbuilding and repair establishments. After 1900, Iwilei attracted warehousing and manufacturing facilities, developing into the city's first large industrial area.

The earliest planned area devoted to such uses was the Airport Industrial Park, a 133-acre area next to Honolulu International Airport that was first occupied by tenants in 1956.

Hawaii State Dept. of Business, Economic Development & Tourism, *State of Hawaii Directory of Industrial and Technology Parks 1991* (1990): 16, 18, 26.

Insurance

On June 12, 1852, *The Polynesian* ran a brief notice signaling the appointment of Dr. Gerrit Parmele Judd as the Honolulu representative of the New England Mutual Life Insurance Company of Boston, thereby making him Hawai'i's first insurance agent of record. The first policy, issued on his own life, was dated October 17, 1851.

Starkey, Janion & Company, a forerunner of Theo. H. Davies & Company, Ltd., became the first agency to write fire insurance in the Islands on December 20, 1855.

Group health insurance was introduced to Hawai'i on June 1, 1938, when the Hawaii Medical Service Association established a plan for schoolteachers and social workers. Coverage was soon opened to industrial groups of five or more employees and their dependents, and in 1946 it was extended to the neighbor islands.

In 1974, the state legislature passed the Hawaii Prepaid Health Care Act, which made Hawai'i the first state in the country to require employers to provide health insurance for their workers. This pioneering law was followed fifteen years later by the State Health Insurance Program Act, which covered about 35,000 persons not yet included under employer-paid policies or Medicaid.

HJH (1980): 84–85; HJH (1988): 233–236; SLH 1974, reg., Act 210; SLH 1989, Act 378; SSB&A, 24 Mar. 1991, B1.

Launderettes

The first self-service laundries opened in Hawai'i in late 1947 or early 1948. Two were listed in the February 1948 telephone directory yellow pages: Launderette at 2031 Kalākaua Avenue and Self Service Laundry at 440 John 'Ena Road. The former advertised itself as "a new, completely automatic, self-service laundry center that washes, triple-rinses and damp-dries up to 9 lbs. of laundry for only 25¢, using the famous BENDIX automatic."

Self-service laundries quickly caught on and within months became a common sight in Honolulu.

Honolulu and Oahu Telephone Directory, February 1948, yellow pages, 57; HA, 26 Sept. 1948, 1–2.

Market Research

The earliest market research firm in Hawai'i, Business Survey and Research Service, was founded by John F. Child, Jr., in 1936. Child was also a key figure in establishing the Hawai'i census tract system (1937), the Hawaii Chapter of the American Statistical Association (1947), and the Hawaii Visitors Bureau research program (1950).

HJH (1987): 116.

Matches

The earliest published Island reference to matches appeared in an advertisement placed by E. & H. Grimes in the *Sandwich Island Mirror & Commercial Gazette* on May 15, 1840. Included in the listing of a vast miscellany of goods carried by the store was a mention of "Lucifer Matches." Not many seem to have been sold; when the 1843 breakdown of imports into the Kingdom was published, only a single case of matches was reported.

SIM, 15 May 1840, 4; F, 1 June 1844, 56–59.

Microwave Ovens

The microwave oven was introduced to Honolulu early in December 1956, when the Hawaiian Electric Company home service staff demonstrated a Hotpoint "electronic cooking center" to amazed newspaper reporters. This showing inaugurated a month-long series of such demonstrations for the general public.

HA, 6 Dec. 1956, B2; HSB, 6 Dec. 1956, 23.

Nylon Hose

"Nylon Hose Now on Sale in Honolulu," proclaimed *The Advertiser*'s headline on May 15, 1940. "Nylon hose has had more pre-sale publicity than any other item in the history of women's wear."

The duPont product was introduced to mainland buyers on the same day.

HA, 15 May 1940, 2–3; Panati (1987): 346; *American Heritage of Invention & Technology*, Fall 1988, 40–55.

Perfumes

Serious efforts to produce perfumes based on Island flowers date at least to the start of the twentieth century. Klu acacia was used in early perfume experiments. Its orange flowers were dipped in coconut oil or cocoa butter and then dried for use in sachets. A 1902 attempt to make perfume from the klu bean failed to prosper, however, because gathering the blossoms from the acacia's sharp-thorned bushes was difficult.

In the 1920s, Hans Bode's Royal Hawaiian Laboratories used Hawaiian plants to produce medicines, soaps, and cosmetics, some of which were perfumed.

The first commercial perfume successfully made in Hawai'i from local Island flowers was introduced in January 1935 at the Gump's department store in Waikīkī. The perfumes available were *pīkake*, pink plumeria, and fern lei, each sold in hand-carved wood bottles.

A, May-June 1989, 27–31; HSB, 9 Mar. 1935, 3; HA, 7 Mar. 1937, 12.

Plumbers

The first plumber in Hawai'i, G. Segelken, arrived in 1850 and opened a shop on Nu'uanu Avenue near the waterfront. Other plumbers soon followed.

In 1861, a newspaper advertisement announced that George C. Riders had "secured the services of a Practical Plumber" and was offering "an assortment of . . . Wash Basins . . . Iron Bath Tubs." The 1869 directory listed three plumbing firms in Honolulu.

HJH (1982): 151.

Printing

Printing was introduced on January 7, 1822, in a grass-roofed hut on the mission grounds about half a mile from the village of Honolulu. The press was an old Ramage model of iron and mahogany, hauled around Cape Horn in the brig *Thaddeus*. Twenty-year-old Elisha Loomis composed two pages of type for an elementary spelling book, and Chief Keeaumoku of Maui made the first impression.

Five hundred copies of the spelling book, called *Ka Pi-a-pa* or *Ka Bi-a-ba* (The alphabet), were issued by the end of January. Originally appearing in sixteen pages, the primer was soon reduced to eight because of a shortage of paper.

The first printed government document, dated March 8, 1822, consisted of two "notices" proclaiming royal laws to control the behavior of sailors and other foreigners.

On December 9, 1824, the first commercial printing job took place when the mission press ran off 220 blank bills of lading for Dixie Wilds, a merchant.

The first lithographic press in Hawai'i—and the Pacific—was installed at the Lahainaluna printing plant in 1846.

Four-color printing was introduced with *The Mid-Pacific Magazine*'s August 1911 issue cover, which was printed in *The Advertiser*'s engraving department. (See also *Books* under AMUSEMENTS AND DIVERSIONS, *Music Printing* under ART AND MUSIC, and *Newspapers* under COMMUNICATION.)

HJH (1979): 108–109; PCA, 15 July 1911, 2.

Refrigeration

The first ice brought to the Islands arrived September 14, 1850, from Boston by way of San Francisco aboard the brig *Fortunio*. On June 22, 1852, a few tons of ice were brought from San Francisco by the bark *Harriet T. Bartlet* and partly sold at auction. The first full cargo of ice came from Sitka aboard the brig *Noble* in the latter part of 1853.

Locally manufactured ice was put on sale in December 1871, but the firm providing it went out of business a month later. Local production of ice was eventually resumed in 1875.

In 1922, the Hawaiian Electric Company imported Kelvinators, the first home electric refrigerators sold in Hawai'i, for testing, but the company did not advertise them until 1924.

Quick-frozen foods initially entered the Island market in 1938, when Rawley's Ice Cream Company ordered its first shipment of Birdseye frosted foods. By 1939, the company had difficulty meeting demand for the products.

HJH (1980): 93; HJH (1993): 240.

Restaurants

Wm. K. Warren has been described as Honolulu's first restaurateur. In 1819, he obtained property at what is now Hotel and Bethel Streets, and around 1825, he built a structure referred to as the Warren House or Major Warren's Hotel. Warren's establishments in Honolulu and California were reportedly famous for their cuisine.

Butler's Coffee House, opened by John Butler in Warren Square, Honolulu, in September 1836, appears to have been the first such establishment in the Islands. It featured spruce beer along with its food.

George C. Knapp and Elwood L. Christensen opened the earliest drive-in restaurant, the KC Drive Inn, in 1927 at the corner of Kalākaua Avenue and Ala Wai Boulevard.

The first pizzeria on Oʻahu apparently made its debut in 1950, when the Little Joe Spaghetti House on Alakea Street advertised, "Spaghetti, Ravioli, Pizza, Mozzarella/Take Out Orders a Specialty/ Please bring your own containers."

La Ronde, later known as Windows of Hawaii, was the state's first revolving restaurant. Located on the twenty-third floor of the Ala Moana Building on Kapiʻolani Boulevard, it opened to the public on November 21, 1961.

HJH (1980): 81; HJH (1981): 108; HJH (1987): 156; SIG, 17 Sept. 1836, 3; Honolulu Telephone Directory for 1950 (yellow pages, 129) and 1960 (yellow pages, 347).

Retail Business

Trade gradually developed during the first two decades of the nineteenth century. Soon after 1800, the king and a few chiefs and foreign settlers were supplying the demands of shipping. After 1812, representatives of various trading houses were regularly stationed at Honolulu. At Waimea, Kaua'i, the plan for the Russian-American Company fort erected in 1817 included a "trading house."

One early trader, James Hunnewell, recalled later that in 1817 and 1818 "all trade was in barter, for there was no money in circulation among the natives. We were the only traders onshore at Honolulu who had any goods to sell. All our cash amounted to $104, and this was received from an English captain and his officers."

In 1823, four American-owned stores, were doing a combined business of $100,000 a year, mostly in barter.

HJH (1980): 80.

Sewing Machines

A major factor in the growth of the garment industry in Hawai'i was the introduction of the sewing machine in 1853. A merchant tailor, J. H. McColgan, brought the first machines from New York on September 12 of that year.

HAA 1896: 67.

Shopping Centers

Planned, integrated shopping centers were first constructed in Hawai'i during the late 1940s and early 1950s. The first such development, the Aloha Shopping Center, opened in 1947 on a 0.75-acre site on Farrington Highway, Waipahu. This modest beginning contained only nine stores, a building area of 6,000 square feet, and fifty parking spaces.

The Aloha Shopping Center, opened in 1947 in Waipahu, was the first of many shopping malls built after World War II. Unlike most later developments, it contained only nine stores and 50 parking spaces. Waipahu Cultural Garden Park.

In 1950, the Aina Haina Shopping Center opened at 820 West Hind Drive, Honolulu, occupying a ten-acre site and including thirty stores, 86,722 square feet of building area, and 203 parking spaces.
HJH (1980): 82.

Strikes

The earliest recorded strike in Hawai'i occurred at Kōloa Plantation on Kaua'i in July 1841, when native laborers struck for higher wages. The plantation management maintained that the workers were well off, receiving *kalo* (taro) lands and housing, fish and poi on working days, freedom from taxes, and a daily wage of twelve and a half cents paid in goods. When their demands for a twenty-five- or fifty-cent daily wage were rejected, the workers returned to work after a week or two.
HJH (1980): 93.

Sugar Production

Sugar cane was among the food crops brought to Hawai'i by its early Polynesian settlers. This cane was not processed but was eaten by chewing the juicy stalks.

Attempts to manufacture sugar in the Islands during the first third of the nineteenth century were limited in scale and generally unsuccessful. The earliest seems to have occurred on Lāna'i in 1802, when a Chinese man supposedly set up a stone mill and boilers, ground off one small crop, and made it into sugar.

A fairly ambitious trial was initiated in 1825, when John Wilkinson and Governor Boki started a plantation in upper Mānoa Valley. Within six months they had seven acres of cane growing, and by September 1826, they had manufactured some sugar. The sugar mill was later converted into a distillery for rum, prompting Kaahumanu, the wife of Kamehameha, to have the cane fields destroyed around 1829.

The first permanent sugar plantation in the Hawaiian Islands was established at Kōloa, Kaua'i, in 1835, by the American mercan-

The Kōloa Plantation was established in 1835 as Hawai'i's first permanent sugar plantation. This 1841 view is from Ronald Takaki's Pau Hana. *(1983).*

tile firm of Ladd and Company. Operations began at Kōloa in the fall under the direction of William Hooper. On May 28, 1836, Hooper wrote that "Mr. French made a shipt. per *Don* of 8000 lb. Sugar and abt. as many galls. Molasses," possibly the earliest export of sugar from the Islands.

The sugar plantations were responsible for several technological innovations, including irrigation and fertilizer. The first extensive use of irrigation was on the Lihue planatation on Kaua'i. In 1856, William H. Rice, manager of the plantation, supervised the digging of a ten-mile-long irrigation ditch and tunnels.

Manure was used as fertilizer on the Lihue plantation beginning in the early 1860s.

HJH (1980): 85–86; HJH (1985): 17–34; HJH (1993): 242.

Tourism Promotion

Although individual hotels, steamship companies, and other firms serving travelers had advertised Hawai'i's visitor attractions for many years, no cooperative, industry-wide effort was made until August 1892 when Lorrin A. Thurston founded the short-lived Hawaiian Bureau of Information.

In January 1903, a Joint Tourist Committee was formed. Upon receiving a $15,000 appropriation from the territorial legislature, this group changed its name to the Hawaii Promotion Committee, and on August 1, 1903, it opened its first office. After several additional name changes, the organization became the Hawaii Visitors Bureau in October 1945.

HJH (1980): 83.

Undertakers

The first known professional undertaker in Hawai'i was C. E. Williams. In 1859, he opened a furniture and mortuary business on Fort Street in Honolulu. (See also *Cemeteries* under BUILDINGS AND AMENITIES.)

The Sales Builder, Mar. 1940, 14.

Unions

The first labor organization in Hawai'i, the Hawaiian Mechanics' Benefit Union, was chartered under the laws of the monarchy on September 1, 1857. It functioned as a mutual benefit society until it was disincorporated on May 25, 1893.

There is no record of a real trade union in Hawai'i until August 9, 1884, when a charter was issued to Typographical Union No. 37 in Honolulu. Seafaring unions, such as the Sailors' Union of the Pacific and the Masters, Mates and Pilots, were also known in the Islands before annexation.

Johannessen (1956): 55–56.

Whaling Ships

Hulsart's 1833 drawing of whalers in Hawaiian waters. Whaleships first appeared in Hawai'i in 1819. AH.

The first whaling ships to visit Hawai'i were the *Balena* (or *Balaena*) out of New Bedford, Massachusetts, commanded by Captain Edmund Gardner, and the 262-ton ship *Equator* from Nantucket (or Newburyport), Massachusetts, with Captain Elisha Folger as skipper. The two vessels arrived via California, anchoring in Kealakekua Bay on September 29, 1819. The first whaling ship to enter Honolulu Harbor was the *Maro*, of Nantucket registry, under Joseph Allen in 1820.

HJH (1979): 99.

Zippers

The slide fastener popularly known as the zipper was first patented in 1893 but did not prove commercially successful. A greatly improved version was patented in 1913 and received its first extensive application in 1917 when used by the U.S. Army and Navy.

The first zippers to reach Hawai'i probably came as part of a 1917 military shipment, intended for use at Schofield Barracks or Pearl Harbor.

Zippers began to appear on civilian clothing during the 1920s and on men's trousers in 1935. The name "zipper" was first applied in 1923, when B. F. Goodrich introduced rubber galoshes equipped with the fastener.

The earliest Honolulu newspaper advertisement to mention zippers was a Liberty House ad for "purses or shopping bags . . . zipper closing," published in December 1929.

Robertson (1974): 209; Kane (1981): 257; Panati (1987): 316–317; *The New Encyclopaedia Britannica*, 15th ed. (Chicago: Encyclopaedia Britannica, Inc., 1991), vol. 12, p. 923; HSB, 23 Dec. 1929, 5.

Office Aids

Abacuses

The abacus was known in Hawai'i by 1842. Sir George Simpson, visiting the Islands that year, remarked that the Chinese shop owners "keep their accounts with a wonderful degree of exactness, making all their calculations by means of an abacus."

Simpson (1847), II: 151–152.

Adding Machines

The adding machine was first sold in Hawai'i about 1896. A. V. Gear advertised the Comptometer early that year. The Burroughs Adding Machine appeared in 1904.

HJH (1980): 89.

Hawai'i's first desk calculator, a Marchant imported in 1911 or 1912, is shown here with Ethel H. Biven, daughter of the man who introduced the machine to Hawai'i. Photographed by the author at Wright, Harvey & Wright in 1965.

Calculators

Fred R. Harvey obtained the earliest desk calculator in the Islands, a hand-cranked Marchant, when he became the first local distributor of Marchant Calculators toward the end of 1911 or beginning of 1912. This machine was still in operating condition in the office of Wright, Harvey, & Wright in 1965.

Electronic desk calculators manufactured by Friden, Marchant, and Wang were available in Honolulu by 1966. Five years later, in June 1971, the Shirokiya department store advertised the first electronic pocket calculator to be sold in the Islands, the Sharp Compet ELSI-8, for $345. (See also *Adding Machines* and *Computers*.)

HJH (1980): 89–90; 74th Annual Report, HHS, 1965: 17–28.

Cash Registers

The city directory first listed cash registers in 1898. Manufactured by the National Cash Register Company, they were distributed in Hawai'i by J. T. Waterhouse.

Hawai'i's earliest talking, computer-assisted, scanning cash register was an R. C. Allen talking register, installed in December 1981 at the Honolulu International Airport newsstand of Makaala, Inc.

Husted's Directory and Hand-Book of Honolulu and the Hawaiian Islands [1899]: 213, 497; HA, 3 Mar. 1982, A1, A4; HA, 5 Mar. 1982, A6.

Computers

The first electronic computer in Hawai'i, the IBM 650, was installed in the Honolulu offices of Libby, McNeill & Libby in November 1956. The first federal agency to operate a computer (also an IBM 650) was the U.S. Army Hawaiian Army Base Command in

July 1957. In April 1960, the University of Hawai'i Statistical and Computing Center received the first computer installed in a state or county agency, again an IBM 650.

The large mainframe computers used in the 1960s were eventually joined—and often supplanted—by minicomput-

The first computer installed in the Islands was an IBM 650, shown at Libby, McNeill & Libby in 1956. Isaiah "Ike" Shon, Libby's computer ace, sits at the console. Libby, McNeill & Libby photo.

ers and microcomputers. Minicomputers began to appear in telephone directory advertisements in 1971 and microcomputers in 1977.

Personal computers and computer stores emerged in the late 1970s. When the *Oahu Telephone Directory* first carried a classified business category for computer stores, in its 1979 edition, it listed ten such establishments. Several more years passed before personal computers began to appear in newspaper display ads. In June 1982, Shirokiya offered the Texas Instruments Home Computer Model TI-99/44 for $525.

Computers were first linked to one another by telephone and radio in the mid-1960s. In 1965, the Federal Communications Commission authorized the Hawaiian Telephone Company to furnish Data-Phone service between Hawai'i and the mainland.

This service, with successive improvements, became Datatel in 1969 and Dasnet on January 3, 1978. Dasnet (for Data Switching Network) allowed Hawai'i-based computers to communicate with more than 175 host computers and thousands of terminals linked to the Telenet mainland network. Unlike earlier services, it permitted the computers and terminals used in one system to interconnect with the computers and terminals of another.

On-line computer-based bibliographic searching came to Hawai'i in the 1970s. The earliest large-scale service of this type available in the Islands appears to have been MEDLINE, offered through the Hawaii Medical Library beginning in mid-July 1973. At that time, MEDLINE contained 500,000 citations to articles in approximately 1,000 medical journals in the National Library of Medicine.

Another important development of the 1970s was the collection of detailed data on the surface of the earth by the LANDSAT Remote Sensor. LANDSAT, first launched in July 1972, is an unmanned, polar earth-orbiting satellite that obtains and transmits information on surface conditions to receiving stations on the ground. Stored in digital form on computer tapes, the data can be converted to photographic format. Between 1974 and 1978, Hawai'i investigated possible local uses of the LANDSAT imagery.

74th Annual Report, HHS, 1965: 17–28; HJH (1980): 90; *Oahu Telephone Directory* for 1 Dec. 1971 (yellow pages, p. 180), 1 Dec. 1977 (yellow pages, p. 227), 1 Dec. 1979 (yellow pages, p. 234); HA, 19 June 1982, A7; HJH (1979): 115.

Copy Machines

Office copying machines became available in Hawai'i in the mid-1950s. Kodak Hawaii, Ltd., was selling the Kodak Verifax printer and materials at least as early as March 1956. The 3M Thermo-Fax "Secretary" was announced two months later. Haloid Xerox copiers and Xerography supplies were advertised locally by 1959.

HJH (1980): 90.

Facsimile Transmissions

Although facsimile received relatively limited use before the 1970s, its history goes back many years. Hawai'i became involved in 1925 when the first transpacific and transcontinental facsimile transmission was made on May 6 from Honolulu to Kahuku by wire, to California by radio, and eventually to New York City by wire. Receiving equipment was still unavailable in Hawai'i at that time.

Fax machines became commercially available in Honolulu at least as early as 1966, when the *Oahu Telephone Directory* yellow pages first carried a rubric for facsimile communication equipment. The sole entry in this category was Harkom Hawaii Inc., authorized distributor for Telautograph.

Yellow page listings for facsimile transmission services were added in 1974, when Louise E. Haller & Associates Inc. was the only firm so classified.

Compact, low-cost units were introduced in the 1980s. This development finally put fax machines within the reach of small businesses and personal users.

HJH (1979): 113–114; H, Oct. 1992, 22; Kane (1981): 526; HSB, 7 May 1925, 1, 3; *Oahu Telephone Directory* for 1 Dec. 1966 (yellow pages, p. 182) and 1 Dec. 1974 (yellow pages, p. 248).

Microfilm

Microfilming, a nineteenth-century invention common on the mainland from the mid-1930s, was introduced to Hawai'i at the approach of World War II. Early in 1941, the Territorial Archives microfilmed its most valuable records and sent copies to mainland depositories for safekeeping.

Bulky newspaper files were prime candidates for microfilming. In 1945, the Library of Hawaii purchased microfilms of the *New York Times*, 1921–1930, and discarded its paper copies. The first Island newspapers to be microfilmed were *The Advertiser*, *The Polynesian*, and the *Star-Bulletin* in the early 1950s.

Robertson (1974): 223–224, 241; Chester R. Young, *The Origin and Development of the Public Archives of Hawaii* (M.A. thesis, University of Hawai'i, 1964): 116; HA, 12 Feb. 1942, 5; HA, 8 June 1947, PM ed., 6; Chieko Tachihata, *The History and Development of Hawaii Public Libraries* (Ph.D. dissertation, University of Southern California, 1981): 236; *Report of the Public Libraries, 1945–1949, Territory of Hawaii*: 8, 17; HHR, July 1966, 332–334.

Mimeography

Duplicating machines employing a typewriter stencil became commercially available in 1888. They were brought to Hawai'i at least as early as 1891, when T. W. Hobron began advertising the Edison Mimeograph.

Robertson (1974): 52; PCA, 13 Oct. 1891, 3.

Punch Card Machines

The first punch card equipment in Hawai'i consisted of IBM 011 Card Punches, a 080 Sorter, and a 285 Tabulator installed in the offices of the Hawaiian Pineapple Company (now Dole Corporation) in November 1930.

Similar equipment was installed by the Bureau of Vital Statis-

An IBM 080 Sorter, the type that brought punchcard tabulation to Hawai'i, is shown at the Hawaiian Pineapple Co. offices in 1930. IBM photo.

tics of the Territorial Board of Health on October 31, 1931, and by the Honolulu Police Department (as a direct result of the Massie murder case) in May 1932.

74th Annual Report, HHS, 1965: 17–28.

Slide Rules

Slide rules came into use in Hawai'i at least as early as 1840. The first issue of *The Polynesian*, published in that year, carried an advertisement for Henry Paty & Company that listed such a device.

P, 6 June 1840, 4.

Typewriters and Word Processors

Messrs. Dillingham & Company received the first typewriter in the Islands—a Remington—in August 1875. By 1895, the machines were more common; forty-six typewriters were imported that year.

The Auto-Typist, a precursor of the modern word processor, was available in Honolulu as early as 1962. The IBM Magnetic Tape/Selectric Typewriter, described as the first modern word processor, was produced in 1964 and introduced to Hawai'i soon afterwards. By 1974, the *Oahu Telephone Directory* included a rubric for word processing equipment and contained its first ads for more advanced IBM and Savin machines. (See also *Computers.*)

HAA 1897: 8; HAA 1909: 138; *New Encyclopaedia Britannica*, 15th ed. (1985), vol. 12, p. 751; *Oahu Telephone Directory* for 1962 (yellow pages, p. 463) and 1 Dec. 1974 (yellow pages, pp. 651, 698, 728).

Government and Social Services

Archives

Completed August 23, 1906, the Territorial Archives Building was the first building in the United States erected solely for the preservation of public archives. A new archives structure replaced the old one in July 1953, and the original building was

The Territorial Archives Building completed in 1906 was a national first. AH.

devoted to other purposes. Both buildings remain standing on the grounds of Iolani Palace.

Chester Raymond Young, *The Origin and Development of the Public Archives of Hawai'i: A Study in Administrative History* (M.A. thesis, University of Hawai'i, 1964): 51, 147.

Army Posts

The first U.S. Army camp in the Islands was Camp McKinley, established in Kapi'olani Park by the newly arrived First New York Volunteer Infantry Regiment on August 16, 1898, just four days after the formal annexation of Hawai'i.

The first permanent U.S. Army post was Kahauiki Military Reservation, established in Honolulu in 1905. Two years later, it was renamed to honor Major General William R. Shafter.

U.S. Army Museum, Hawai'i, exhibit captions.

Camp McKinley was erected in Kapi'olani Park in 1898 to house American armed forces en route to the Philippines during the war with Spain. AH.

Censorship

Censorship of the press first became an issue in 1838, only four years after the founding of Hawai'i's earliest newspapers. The Reverend Reuben Tinker, the editor of *Ke Kumu Hawaii*, became dissatisfied with the policy of the American Board of Commissioners for Foreign Missions (ABCFM) from Boston, which censored materials for publication. He severed all ties with ABCFM in 1838 and soon left Hawai'i.

The Provisional Government was responsible for the first official censorship of newspapers. On January 30, 1893, only thirteen days after the overthrow, the Provisional Government legislature enacted a law forbidding "seditious libel," which it defined as any published statement intended "to bring into hatred or contempt, or to excite disaffection against the Provisional Government." A year later, this statute was made part of the 1894 constitution of the Republic of Hawai'i. Numerous suits were filed against newspapers and their editors and printers, notably the royalist and bilingual *Ka Holomua* (The progressive). The Provisional Government suspended *Ka Holomua* and sent several editors and printers to jail.

Books, pictures, and theatrical performances were censored beginning in the 1850s. The Penal Code of 1850 banned "any obscene picture, or pamphlet, sheet or other thing containing obscene language, obscene prints, figures, descriptions or representations."

HJH (1994): 157–161.

Censuses

Sometime around A.D. 1500, Umi, king of the Big Island, supposedly conducted a census of his realm. Collecting all his people on a plain near Hualālai, he instructed each person to deposit a stone on the pile representing his district.

The first population census in historical times was undertaken in Wainiha Valley, Kaua'i, near the beginning of the nineteenth century. A careful census of the valley counted more than 2,000 people, sixty-five of whom were described as *menehune*. *Menehune* were the legendary race of small people who worked at night building fish ponds, roads, and temples.

The first full-scale censuses, covering all the Islands, were made under missionary auspices in 1831 and 1832 and in 1835 and 1836. The first of these counts reported a total population of 130,313; the second found only 108,579.

The earliest census conducted by the Hawaiian government to achieve reasonably complete coverage was undertaken in January 1850, when enumerators found only 84,165 persons living in the Kingdom. Depopulation continued until 1876, when the total reached 53,900.

Since 1900, the U.S. Bureau of the Census has made decennial counts. The population numbered 154,001 in 1900, 422,770 in 1940, 964,691 in 1980, and 1,108,229 in 1990.

HAA 1917: 63; HAA 1913: 125–137; *American Statistician*, Feb. 1981, 1–3; Schmitt (1973): 8; Schmitt (1968): 69, 223; SHDB 1992: 12.

Chief Executives

Hawai'i's chief executives have held a variety of titles: king or queen from 1795 to 1893, president from 1893 to 1900, and governor from 1900 to the present.

The first monarch to rule all the Islands was Kamehameha I. By 1795, Kamehameha had conquered all of the chain except Kaua'i and Ni'ihau, which were ceded to his kingdom in 1810.

Hawai'i's first and only president was Sanford B. Dole. On January 17, 1893, the Committee of Safety, a band of revolu-

Kamehameha I, first ruler of a united Hawai'i, as pictured by Louis Choris in 1816. AH.

The 1900 inauguration of Hawai'i's first governor, Sanford B. Dole. Previously, Dole had served as the first (and only) president of both the Provisional Government and Republic. AH.

tionaries made up primarily of haole businessmen, deposed Queen Liliuokalani, proclaimed the formation of a provisional government, and named Dole its president.

Dole also served as Hawai'i's first territorial governor, a post he was appointed to by President William McKinley. Dole occupied this position from June 14, 1900, when Hawai'i became a U.S. Territory, until November 23, 1903, when he resigned to become a federal judge.

Hawai'i's first elected governor was William F. Quinn, who took office when Hawai'i became a state on August 21, 1959. Quinn was the Territory's last appointed governor, having assumed office September 2, 1957, after his selection by President Dwight Eisenhower.

Daws (1968): 29–60; Kuykendall and Day (1961): 178, 183, 305–306; Kuykendall (1967): 596–597; Ronck (1984): 129.

Civil Service

Limited civil service was authorized by the 1913 territorial legislature. One act, approved April 4, 1913, provided for the appointment of the Honolulu Civil Service Commission, with jurisdiction over the city and county police and fire departments. A second law established a civil service commission covering employees of the territorial Board of Health.

The 1939 legislature put civil service on an island-wide basis. Separate civil service commissions were established for the territorial government and each of its four political subdivisions, and coverage was extended to most territorial and county employees.

From 1917 to 1927, a pension system for police, firemen, and band members existed in Honolulu, offering retirement at half-pay after twenty-five years of service. In 1926, the Employees' Retirement System of the Territory of Hawai'i made retirement permissible for public workers at sixty years of age and compulsory at seventy.

Cost-of-living allowances for federal employees in Hawai'i were authorized in 1940. In January 1943, a uniform pay differential, amounting to 25 percent over comparable mainland scales, was established. This differential has been frequently adjusted and in recent years has varied by island, but is still in effect for federal white-collar employees.

HJH (1980): 97.

Constitutions

On October 8, 1840, King Kamehameha III and his *kuhina-nui* (a very powerful official), Kekauluohi, signed Hawai'i's first constitution. Until then, the Kingdom had been governed as an absolute monarchy. The new constitution created an elected house of representatives and a supreme court. A declaration of rights, often called the Hawaiian Magna Carta, served as a preamble.

The constitution of 1840 was the first of seven such documents to govern Hawai'i during the next 150 years. New constitutions were enacted in 1852, 1864, 1887, and 1894, each one less democratic than its predecessor. As a U.S. Territory, Hawai'i's basic law was the Organic Act, passed by Congress on April 30, 1900.

In 1959, Hawai'i's current constitution (approved by the electorate in 1950) went into effect upon the Territory's formal admission as a state.

Kuykendall (1938): 160, 167–169, 266–267; Kuykendall (1953): 127–134; Kuykendall (1967): 366–372, 649; Kuykendall and Day (1961): 183–184, 194, 297; HRS, 1985 Replacement, vol. 1, 36–85, 97–166.

County Governments

A bill authorizing the establishment of county governments was enacted by the 1903 territorial legislature, but the newly elected county officials held office only two weeks before the territorial supreme court declared the act unconstitutional. The 1905 legislature passed a new county act, which was sustained by the supreme court, and on June 30, the Board of Supervisors of the County of O'ahu was formally sworn in.

The 1907 territorial legislature created the City and County of Honolulu from the County of O'ahu. On January 4, 1909, Mayor Joseph J. Fern and a new Board of Supervisors were inaugurated, and the municipality was officially established.

HJH (1980): 96–97; Johnson (1991): 38–66.

Delegates to Congress

Hawai'i's first delegate to the U.S. Congress was Robert W. Wilcox, a member of the Home Rule Party. In the first territorial

Robert W. Wilcox was elected in 1900 as Hawai'i's first delegate to the U.S. Congress. AH.

election, held November 6, 1900, Wilcox was elected to both the unexpired term of the Fifty-sixth Congress and the full term of the Fifty-seventh Congress. In the 1902 election, Wilcox was defeated by Jonah Kuhio Kalanianaole.

Report of the Governor of the Territory of Hawaii to the Secretary of the Interior for 1901 (p. 67) and 1903 (p. 46).

Education

Classroom education in Hawai'i was initiated by Jean Rives, who in 1810 started a school for Liholiho (the future Kamehameha II) and his four brothers but abandoned it after only three weeks. A more auspicious beginning occurred on May 23, 1820, with the opening of the first Protestant mission school in Honolulu. Two months later, about thirty pupils were under instruction.

The earliest secondary school, Lahainaluna, opened in 1831 as a mission school for the training of teachers and ministers, near Lahaina, Maui.

Public education in Hawai'i dates from October 15, 1840, when

Mrs. Bingham's school—Hawai'i's earliest—as sketched by G. Holmes in 1821. Hawaiian Mission Children's Society Library/Mission Houses Museum.

The entire faculty of the College of Agriculture and Mechanic Arts (predecessor of the University of Hawai'i) in 1909. UH.

Hawai'i Hall was the first building erected on the new Mānoa campus of the University of Hawai'i in 1912. UH.

a law was enacted providing for the establishment of public schools and requiring the attendance of all children four to fourteen years of age.

Public secondary education first became available in the last decades of the nineteenth century. Honolulu High School opened in 1895 when the upper grades of the Fort Street school were moved into the "new" Honolulu High School building (the former Princess Ruth Keelikolani palace). Although public, this school charged tuition until 1899.

The first collegiate instruction in the Islands took place at Punahou (rechartered as Oahu College) when four freshmen enrolled in 1856. By 1865, when college-level courses were discontinued, fourteen students had completed the two-year program and three had transferred to Yale and Williams as juniors.

Public higher education in Hawai'i began with the creation of the College of Agriculture and Mechanic Arts in 1907. In June 1912, four seniors received Bachelor of Science degrees at the first commencement exercises. The college was renamed the College of Hawaii in 1911 and became the University of Hawai'i on July 1, 1920.

The first private four-year college in the Islands was Jackson College, established by the Hawaii Baptist Foundation in Mānoa in 1949. Never accredited, Jackson met its end in a foreclosure sale in October 1965.

HJH (1980): 95–96.

Elections

The first election by ballot took place on January 6, 1851, when representatives were chosen for the Legislative Council scheduled to meet on April 30 of that year.

Many politicians now campaign for office by standing on street curbs, holding banners and waving signs. The first to do so is now thought to have been H. H. Dick Hedlund, who, when running for the territorial house of representatives in 1958, held up a broom with a sign on it at Castle Junction in Windward O'ahu.

HJH (1980): 96; HJH (1971): 53; HSB, 25 Aug. 1992, A12.

Fee Simple Land Ownership

Until the 1840s, all land in Hawai'i belonged to the king. This system was drastically altered by legislation that established a board of commissioners to quiet land titles (enacted in 1845), permitted fee simple ownership for Hawaiian subjects (1846), and extended similar rights to aliens (1847 and 1850). The first Mahele, dividing the land between the king and chiefs, was signed on January 27, 1848.

Early in 1846, however, the government decided to experiment with fee simple ownership without waiting for the new law to go into operation. Nearly 100 parcels of land were sold in the Makawao district on Maui, amounting to 900 acres purchased for one dollar per acre. In Mānoa Valley, O'ahu, about thirty parcels were sold, ranging from one to ten acres, and the buyers were given fee simple titles.

Kuykendall (1938): 269–298.

Fire Departments

The Honolulu Fire Department originated in 1850 when two volunteer companies were organized: Honolulu Company No. 1 and Mechanic Engine Company No. 2.

According to a reminiscence published in 1880, the first fire engine brought to the Islands arrived in 1846 or 1847. The hand engine, owned by a Chinese firm, was small and not very well constructed. Water was bailed into it with buckets.

The first time a fire engine was used in Honolulu was at a fire that broke out at the corner of Maunakea and King Streets. At that time, wells provided the only water supply. Because of the excitement caused by the fire and the use of the new machine, firefighters accidentally laid the suction pipe down a cesspool instead of a well.

The volunteer fire departments eventually achieved professional status. In the 1880s, volunteers were paid according to their

Volunteer Engine Company No. 2's fire chief and his assistant with the company's steam pumper, pictured near the bell tower on Union Street during the 1880s. AH.

rank and the number of fires they attended. On March 1, 1893, a regularly paid fire department was created by an act of the legislature.

HJH (1980): 98–99; The Hawaiian Kingdom Statistical and Commercial Directory and Tourists' Guide. 1880–1881 (Honolulu and San Francisco: George Bowser & Company, 1880): 455.

Generals, Three-Star

Benjamin Webster was the first Islander to achieve three-star rank in the U.S. Armed Forces. Although born in Connecticut, he moved to Hawai'i with his family at the age of two. He graduated from the U.S. Military Academy at West Point in 1932 and went on to become a lieutenant general in the U.S. Air Force before retiring in 1965.

HSB, 16 July 1990, A2.

Government Planning

In 1845, the Hawaiian government employed H. Ehrenberg, a German engineer, to survey the streets and draw a map of Honolulu.

The first official planning agency in Hawai'i, the Honolulu City Planning Commission, was established in 1915. It operated without a staff until 1920, when it was allotted $3,000 for a secretary with a desk in the mayor's office. The first zoning ordinance was approved on April 17, 1922.

The first official planning agency with territorial scope was the Territorial Planning Board, created by the 1937 legislature. It relinquished its functions to the Economic Planning and Coordination Authority in 1955.

The first comprehensive state plan in the country was *The General Plan of the State of Hawaii*, submitted by the State Planning Office to Governor William Quinn in January 1961.

Created in 1961, the State Land Use Commission was the first in the nation with authorization to zone an entire state.

HJH (1980): 99–100.

Kindergartens

Hawai'i's first kindergarten teacher appears to have been Birch Fanning. She arrived in Honolulu on August 3, 1889, and announced her plans "to open a high class kindergarten school, for young children whose parents are able to pay a moderate fee for the tuition." What became of these plans is unknown. Fanning appeared in the 1892 city directory as a "kindergarten teacher, Punahou Prep School." A history of Punahou, without specifying any dates, notes that "for a short time a private kindergarten was set up in a vacant room at the Preparatory," presumably the same facility listed in the 1892 directory. This experiment appears to have been short-lived, and the inception of a permanent kindergarten program at Punahou did not take place until 1900.

The efforts of Francis Damon and a women's association were more successful. Damon established a kindergarten in 1892 in connection with the Chinese Mission of which he had charge. His experiment was so successful that the idea was taken over by the Woman's Board of Missions, which organized four kindergartens in 1893—one each for Japanese, Portuguese, and Hawaiian students, and one for children of other races.

All of the early kindergartens were privately funded, and it was many years before the territorial government entered the field. The 1919 legislature finally provided the necessary money, and public kindergartens were established at Waialua (Oʻahu), Kahului, and Hilo. By June 1921, enrollment totaled 587 on three islands, but a year later it was only fifty-two, all on Kauaʻi. Public kindergarten then disappeared for two decades, not resurfacing until 1943. (See also *Education.*)

PCA, 10 Aug. 1889, 3; *Directory and Hand-Book of the Kingdom of Hawaii* (San Francisco: F. M. Husted, 1892): 128, 435; Alexander and Dodge (1941): 400, 402; Wist (1940): 134, 169–170; HAA 1898: 79; *Report of the Governor of Hawaii to the Secretary of the Interior* for 1920 (p. 60), 1921 (p. 70), and 1922 (p. 67); SLH 1937, Act 155; SLH 1943, Act 220; HSB, 1 Sept. 1943, 1; HSB, 18 Sept. 1943, 11.

Legislatures

Hawaiʻi's first legislature convened on April 1, 1841, at Luaehu, Lahaina, Maui. The nobles met and were joined by three unnamed elected representatives. This legislative council sat for thirty-four days, until May 31.

Robert C. Lydecker, comp., *Roster, Legislatures of Hawaii, 1841–1918* (AH, Pub. no. 1, 1918): 4, 16.

Marriage and Divorce

Before the arrival of Protestant missionaries in the 1820s, marriage and divorce were quite informal in Hawaiʻi. Very little ceremony was connected with marriage, except for people of superior rank.

The first Christian marriage in the Islands took place on August 11, 1822, when Hiram Bingham officiated at the wedding of Thomas Hopu and Delia. In 1826, non-Christian marriage was outlawed on Maui, and shortly afterward this ban was extended to all the Islands. The first laws regarding divorce were proclaimed by Kaahumanu by 1832.

The first marriage between persons of the same sex took place in April 1981. State officials at that time issued a marriage license to two men, but after discovering that the "bride" had male genitals, the officials refused to recognize the marriage.

Adams (1937): 46; *HHR, Selected Readings* (1969): 241; Schmitt (1977): 41, 61; *HA*, 18 Dec. 1990, A4.

Mayors

The 1905 territorial legislature provided for each county to have an elected Board of Supervisors, presided over by a chairman. In 1909, however, O'ahu County was redesignated the City and County of Honolulu, with an elective mayor. Sixty years later, mayoral positions were created for the other counties.

The first mayor of the City and County of Honolulu was Joseph James Fern, who was elected in November 1908. A Democrat, Fern was reelected in 1910, 1912, 1917, and 1919, and defeated in 1914.

Hawai'i's first neighbor island mayors were all Democrats who assumed office in 1969: Shunichi Kimura on the Big Island, Antone K. Vidinha in Kaua'i County, and Elmer F. Cravalho in Maui County.

HJH (1975): 74–100; Ronck (1984): 130; SLH 1905, Act 39, ch. 6, sec. 12, and ch. 18, sec. 81; county charters.

Joseph J. Fern was the first mayor of the City and County of Honolulu. *Photograph from Municipal Reference & Records Center.*

Palaces

King Kamehameha I, the first king to unite all the Hawaiian Islands, lived in several thatched hut "palaces" during his reign. After conquering Oʻahu in 1795, he began to consolidate his kingdom and established his first residence in Waikīkī. In 1809, he moved to Honolulu Harbor, near the canoe landing at Pākākā. The palace, called Halehui, was the largest building in his compound.

The first Hawaiian palace made with permanent materials was constructed in Lahaina, Maui, by "foreigners," around 1800. Built with adobe bricks made from soil in the area, it was then whitewashed for protection from the rain. Kamehameha stayed at this palace whenever he resided at Lahaina.

Iolani Palace, in downtown Honolulu, is the second royal residence to occupy the location. The first was used by Hawaiʻi's monarchs from 1845 to 1879. King Kalakaua, elected in 1874, decided to replace the structure, which had become infested with termites. The present building, completed in 1882, remained Hawaiʻi's official house of state until the monarchy was abolished in 1893.

W. F. Judd (1975): 24–25, 61, 66–95, 118–148; Hackler (1987).

The first Iolani Palace was used by Island monarchs from 1845 to 1879. AH.

Passports

On May 2, 1845, Robert C. Wyllie issued the first passport granted by the Kingdom of Hawai'i. The recipient was Jose Nadal.

AH, file folder, "Passports, No. 1–287, May 2, 1845–Jan. 17, 1849."

Patents

On November 14, 1879, a San Francisco resident, Andrew S. Hallidie, wrote to Samuel G. Wilder, minister of the interior, for a patent on his invention, a method of transporting sugar cane and other substances that consisted of a wire rope carried on pulleys. On February 19, 1880, Hallidie was awarded Hawaiian Patent No. 1 for his efforts.

AH, file folder, "Interior, misc., Patents nos. 1 and 2."

Political Polls

Before World War II, political opinion polls in Hawai'i were typically unscientific and limited in scope. In 1940, for example, *The Honolulu Advertiser* asked readers to mail in their choices for U.S. president. Lacking the right to cast a real vote in such races before statehood, 4,144 readers nonetheless responded.

The earliest large-scale political opinion survey, using modern sampling procedures, appears to have been a study made by Territorial Surveys in August 1948. Two samples were drawn, one of 1,200 adults in all parts of Honolulu and the other of 400 Kaimukī residents. Respondents were predominantly Democratic in their sympathies. Even so, most of them told interviewers they preferred Joseph R. Farrington, a Republican, as delegate to Congress, a finding confirmed in the election that November.

HJH (1987): 120–121.

Presidential Residences

The first—and only—U.S. president to live in Hawai'i was Jimmy Carter. In December 1948, Carter, then a young naval officer, was assigned to Pearl Harbor and the USS *Pourfret*, his first submarine. Until 1951, the future president and his wife, Rosalynn, occupied a two-bedroom apartment at 318 Sixth Street, Hale Moku, close to Nimitz Gate. While there, the two studied Hawaiian history, and Rosalynn took hula lessons.

HSB, 4 Dec. 1976, A1; Mazlish and Diamond (1979): 111–112; Simmons (1979): 33–34.

Presidential Visits

The first U.S. president to visit Hawai'i while in office was Franklin D. Roosevelt, who arrived in Honolulu aboard the cruiser *Houston* on July 26, 1934, and departed two days later.

The first U.S. president to visit the Islands before he reached office was William Howard Taft. Sailing to

Above: President Franklin D. Roosevelt speaking from the lanai of Iolani Palace during his 1934 visit. AH.

Left: William Howard Taft and Alice Roosevelt during Taft's second visit to Hawai'i in 1905. AH.

his new post as governor of the Philippines, Taft and his family spent four days on O'ahu in April 1900. In 1905, Taft (then secretary of war) visited Hawai'i again, accompanied by Theodore Roosevelt's daughter, Alice.

HAA 1935: 39–43; Anderson (1981): 68; *Outrigger Canoe Club Forecast*, Nov. 1951, 4–5; PCA, 10 July 1905, 1–2; F, Aug. 1905, 15.

Social Insurance

The passage of the Workmen's Compensation Act by the 1915 territorial legislature instituted the earliest government-sponsored social insurance program. It compensated employees for personal injuries sustained in the course of their employment.

The enactment of several limited relief programs soon followed. In 1915, the legislature authorized the Board of Immigration, Labor, and Statistics to pay "for the temporary relief of indigent, suffering, and helpless persons." The 1918 special session passed a bill allowing the Honolulu Board of Supervisors to appropriate funds "for the relief of aged and destitute persons." A year later, the legislature created a board of child welfare in each county, empowered to grant allowances to widowed, deserted, or single mothers.

Large-scale government assistance to the unemployed and poor was introduced in 1933 when the Old Age Pension Law was enacted and the Governor's Unemployment Relief Commission was established. Welfare programs, personnel, and budgets were greatly expanded.

The Social Security Act, approved by President Roosevelt on August 14, 1935, also initiated a number of major social insurance programs. One was a federal-state system of unemployment compensation, financed by taxes on employers. Unemployed workers began receiving compensation under this program in January 1939. Another important program established by the Social Security Act was Old-Age and Survivors Insurance, for which monthly payments began in Hawai'i in January 1940.

HJH (1980): 94–95; HJH (1993): 242.

Social Surveys

In the 1840s, Robert Crichton Wyllie conducted the first modern social surveys in the Pacific. The first of his works, a compilation of existing material, was published in *The Friend* from May to December 1844. His second work, issued in 1848, consisted of more than a hundred questions he submitted to missionaries and educators on all the Islands and their often inadequate answers.

HJH (1980): 94; *American Statistician*, Feb. 1981, 3.

Social Welfare

Beginning in the 1820s, Island churches engaged in various charitable activities. The Seaman's Bethel, established by the Reverend John Diell at King and Bethel Streets in 1837, was particularly active, aiding many sailors over the years.

The earliest organization devoted exclusively to social welfare work was the Stranger's Friend Society, formed in 1852 by fifty-two women who aided the sick and destitute. More than a century later, the society was described as the oldest charitable organization west of the Rocky Mountains.

The Bureau of Sight Conservation and Work with the Blind was the first autonomous territorial casework organization supported only by taxation. This agency originated in a 1932 request for help addressed to the National Society for Prevention of Blindness, which led one year later to the appointment of the Governor's Committee on Conservation of Sight and in 1935 to the creation of the bureau itself.

Federated giving in Hawai'i dates to the first United Welfare Campaign, conducted on O'ahu in March 1919. The drive raised $186,000 for seventeen member agencies.

HJH (1980): 94; Catton (1959): 8–9, 114–115.

State Flag

Sometime prior to 1816, a flag was designed for King Kamehameha. This flag has been officially used by the Kingdom, Republic, Territory, and State of Hawai'i for more than 175 years.

Kuykendall (1938): 54–55; Hawaii State Library System, *Names and Insignia of Hawaii* (rev. 1970); HRS, 1992 Supp., sec. 5-19, 5-20.

State Nature Symbols

The 1923 legislature designated the *pua aloalo* or hibiscus the flower emblem of Hawai'i. Initially, no particular color was specified, but in 1988 the legislature named the native yellow hibiscus the official state flower.

On May 7, 1957, the twenty-ninth territorial legislature designated the *nēnē* or Hawaiian goose as the territorial bird. An act of the 1988 legislature officially made it the state bird.

The *kukui* or candlenut tree was designated the official state tree by the thirtieth territorial legislature in 1959. Previously, the *niu* or coconut palm had been the official tree of the Territory, having been designated by Governor Lawrence M. Judd in 1930.

The humpback whale was selected as the state marine mammal by the legislature in 1979.

The 1985 legislature named the *humuhumu-nukunuku-ā-pua'a* the state fish, to serve for a five-year period. As of 1995, no replacement had been chosen.

Hawaii State Library System, *Names and Insignia of Hawaii* (rev. 1970); HRS, 1985 Replacement, vol. 1, sec. 5-8, 5-12, 5-13; SLH 1988, Acts 177, 178; SLH 1985, Act 289, sec. 1; SLH 1979, Act 110.

State Seal

Officially designated by Act 272 of the 1959 territorial legislature, the Great Seal is based on the Territorial Seal (1901), which in turn was derived from the Seal of the Republic (1896). The latter was a modification of the Coat of Arms and Seal of the Kingdom of Hawai'i, adopted in May 1845.

Hawaii State Library System, *Names and Insignia of Hawaii* (rev. 1970); HRS, 1985 Replacement, vol. 1, sec. 5-5.

State Song

"Hawai'i Pono'ī" was the national song of the Hawaiian Kingdom. In 1874, King Kalakaua wrote the lyrics, which were set to music by Captain Henry Berger, bandmaster of the Royal Hawaiian Band. The song was made Hawai'i's national anthem in 1876 and the state anthem in 1967.

Two earlier anthems preceded "Hawai'i Pono'ī" but never received formal recognition. The first was "E Ola Ka Moi," a Hawaiian translation of "God Save the King," drafted in 1862 and set to the same music. The second was "Mele Lāhui Hawai'i," composed by Liliuokalani in 1868 at the request of Kamehameha V.

64th Annual Report, HHS, 1955: 8–10; Hawaii State Library System, *Names and Insignia of Hawaii* (rev. 1970); SLH 1967, Act 301; HRS, 1985 Replacement, sec. 5-10.

Taxation

Taxation in eighteenth-century Hawai'i took the form of tribute exacted from the common people. During the *makahiki* season, a four-month period commencing in October or November, a figure of the god Lono was paraded around each of the Islands. At each district boundary, the bearers of the god-image stopped to receive the people's tribute, which would support the temples, priesthood, and nobles.

By 1823, this tribute had become an annual rent tax, sometimes paid in Spanish dollars and, at other times, in sandalwood.

Income was not taxed until 1894. The law applied a one-percent levy on income resulting from economic activity within the Republic. A family exemption of $2,000 was allowed if total personal income did not exceed $4,000. Declared unconstitutional, this law was replaced in 1901 with a two-percent tax on both personal and corporate income. An exemption of $1,000 was provided for all families, regardless of size. At the time the 1901 law was passed, the only American state with an income tax in force was Virginia.

Kamins (1952): 154–179; SLH 1896, Act 65; Campbell v. Shaw (1897) 11 Hawai'i 112; SLH 1901, Act 20.

Thrones

In 1847, Kamehameha III commissioned Christian and Johann La Frenz to design and build the first throne of the Hawaiian monarchy period. Completed on November 27 at a cost of $138, the upholstered throne was made of koa with double-reeded arms and cabriole legs and was surmounted by a carved crown, an adopted western symbol of the monarchy. The throne now rests in the Bishop Museum.

Jenkins (1983): 105–106.

U.S. Senators and Representatives

Upon achieving statehood in 1959, Hawai'i was awarded two seats in the U.S. Senate and a single seat in the U.S. House of Representatives. In the July 28, 1959, election, Hiram L. Fong, a Republican, and Oren E. Long, a Democrat, won the Senate seats, and Daniel K. Inouye, a Democrat, took the House seat.

Kuykendall and Day (1961): 303; Ronck (1984): 129; Schmitt (1977): 604–605.

War Veterans

War veterans were common among the ancient Hawaiians. For centuries before Kamehameha, the different island chiefs frequently engaged in contests over land or battles of revenge.

Veterans of U.S. conflicts first appeared in Hawai'i in the early nineteenth century (perhaps even the 1790s), but most of them were mainlanders who had migrated to the Islands long after their military service. It was not until World War I that the U.S. armed forces included a large number of people actually born in the Islands.

The Revolutionary War ended only a few years after Captain James Cook's voyage, so it is extremely unlikely that any native Hawaiians participated in it. A few early haole residents could conceivably have been veterans of that war, however. One frequent Island visitor with such credentials was John Kendrick, a privateering captain in the Revolution, who died in Honolulu in 1794.

The first Hawai'i-born veteran of a major U.S. conflict may have been a son of John Young who apparently saw service with the U.S. Navy in the War of 1812. Charles Barnard, an Island visitor near the end of that war, quoted Young as telling him, "I have a son, who has just returned from the United States, who is a good seaman, and has been on board an armed vessel, fighting for free trade and sailors' rights."

A more controversial claimant to being the first Island native in an American war is George Prince Tamoree, the son of the last king of Kaua'i. Also known as Humehume and George Prince Kaumualii, George wrote to his father on October 19, 1816:

> I went to Boston and listed in the U. States servis [sic] and I shipped on board the brig *Enterprise* in order to go and fight with the Englishmen. . . . We fought with her [the *Boxer*] about an hour and in the mean time, I was wounded in my right side with a boarding pike, which it pained me very much.

Later, George continued, he served on the *Guerrier* [*Guerriere*], fighting at Algiers and Tripoly [sic].

George's account has been accepted by some historians and disputed by others. According to U.S. Navy records, George did not enlist until June 21, 1815, six months after the Treaty of Ghent was signed, ending the war. These same records show that the young prince, who first served on the *Enterprise*, later transferred to the *Guerriere*, from which he was eventually discharged on March 25, 1816. Thus, his time in uniform was entirely postwar.

Handy et al. (1965): 233; Day (1984): 76; Barnard (1829): 233; *55th Annual Report, HHS, 1946*: 8–9; F, Oct. 1940, 188, 192; *41st Annual Report, HHS, 1932*: 47; PP, June 1940, 16; HJH (1981): 33.

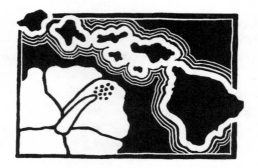

Crime and Justice

Crime Statistics

The first known statistics on criminal justice referred to the number of convictions by type of offense for Honolulu in 1838. The most common offense was adultery, accounting for 246 of the 522 convictions. The most serious was manslaughter, with four cases.

HHR, *Selected Readings* (1969): 234.

Fingerprinting

The earliest recorded use of fingerprinting for identification purposes in Hawai'i occurred in 1896, some thirty-eight years after the practice was pioneered by William Herschel in India.

Act 13 of the 1896 legislature required all male residents of the Republic, fifteen years and older, to register with the government

National Register of the Republic of Hawaii
CERTIFICATE OF REGISTRATION

No. 541
District of _Honolulu_, Island of _Oahu_

THIS IS TO CERTIFY, that on this _12_ day of _May_ 1896, _James A. King_ has registered in this district.

A description of said person is as follows:

Age _63_
Country of birth _Scotland_
Residence _Emma St_
Port of departure for the Republic of Hawaii: _San Francisco_
Date of arrival here _Dec 1889_
Married or single _Married_
Occupation _Minister of Interior_
Location of Occupation _Executive Bldgs._
Name of employer _Haw'n Gov't._
Residence of employer _____
Distinguishing marks of features _Ht 5 ft 10 in Wht 200 lbs. hair iron gray eyes. blue scar over left eye._
Thumb mark: _Features Full_

Jonathan Shaw
Superintendent Registrar.
District of _Honolulu,_
Island of _Oahu._

Fingerprinting in Hawai'i goes back at least as far as 1896, when all males 15 years and older were required to register and affix their thumb mark to a registration form. This is James King's registration.

and specified that the registration form was to include the registrant's "thumb mark." Less than eight weeks later, this law was repealed by the same legislative session, but not before a number of compliant males had duly completed the forms and affixed their thumbprints. Island police departments probably adopted fingerprinting for criminal detection soon after 1917. In that year, the territorial legislature passed Act 178, "to provide for the establishment of systems for the identification of criminals." The act appropriated $3,000 to establish "the finger print system and the Bertillon system in and at the Territorial prison and such other of the various jails and places of detention."

The Automated Fingerprint Identification System, a computerized fingerprint matching system, was installed at the Hawaii Criminal Justice Data Center in August 1990.

Robertson (1974): 72–73; Kane (1981): 262; SLH 1896, Act 31, sec. 10; SLH 1896, Act 76; SLH 1917, Act 178; HA, 25 Aug. 1990, A1, A8.

Judiciary

The earliest signs of a formal judiciary appeared in 1828. Kaahumanu, the wife of Kamehameha I, informed the missionaries of the "appointment of a number of persons to investigate cases and try causes." In 1829, the governor of Kaua'i appointed five persons to positions comparable to that of a "justice of the peace in America."

Hawai'i's constitution of 1840 created a six-member supreme court—the Kingdom's first—to consist of the king, the *kuhina-nui*, and four judges appointed by the "representative body" (legislature). An "Act to Organize the Judiciary Department," passed September 7, 1847, assigned much of the work of the supreme court to a new body, the Superior Court of Law Equity. The two courts were eventually combined, as a single supreme court, by the constitution of 1852.

The first chief justice was William Little Lee, who took his oath of office in 1848 and served until his death in 1857.

Kuykendall (1938): 129, 167–168, 263–264, 268; Kuykendall (1953): 37; Ronck (1984): 131.

Laws and Lawyers

Hawai'i's first printed laws were issued March 8, 1822. They pertained to foreigners disturbing the peace and sailors deserting their ships.

Trained lawyers remained unknown in Hawai'i until the arrival of John Ricord on February 27, 1844. Ricord received his legal education in New York. As the only attorney in the Kingdom, he was appointed attorney general within eleven days of his arrival and remained in that post until 1847.

The first lawyer in private practice in Hawai'i was Richard Ford, "conveyancer and attorney" (and also a physician), who arrived in August 1844. Soon afterward, he opened a law office.

Hawai'i's earliest woman lawyer was Almeda Eliza Hitchcock

(1863–1895). A native of Hilo who attended the University of Michigan, she was admitted to the bar there December 27, 1887, and to the Hawaii Bar upon her return to Hilo the following year.

HJH (1980): 96, 98; HJH (1986): 137–150.

Police

The first police force in Hawai'i consisted of guards in the service of Kamehameha I and some of his senior chiefs. These guards, called *ilimuku* or *kula'ilua*, were organized sometime before 1810.

In 1831, under Governor Kuakini, the police were required to patrol the village daily, enforcing the Sabbath laws and other moral strictures.

The present-day Honolulu Police Department traces its origins to 1834, when Kamehameha III organized the first police force. Other sources place the date in 1840, when Kamehameha III signed into law a new set of statutes, which, among other provisions, authorized the Island governors to appoint police officers and constables "for the protection of the people and villages." The same law also provided for a badge to identify officers and constables—"a stick made round at one end with the name of the king on it."

HJH (1980): 97–98.

Prisons

Honolulu Fort, erected alongside the harbor at the foot of Fort Street in 1816, served as the Kingdom's first prison. This use was first officially proclaimed in two edicts issued by Kamehameha II on March 8, 1822. One specified that "should any seaman of whatever vessel, be found riotous or disturbing the peace in any manner, he or they shall be immediately secured in the Fort." The other provided similar treatment for disorderly resident foreigners.

The fort continued to be used as a prison—and insane asylum—until 1857, when it was dismantled.

The first capital punishment was administered in the fort in 1840, when Chief Kamanawa was hanged for poisoning Kamokuiki.

F, May 1935, 503; HJH (1968): 4; W. F. Judd (1975): 41, 46–47, 50.

Reformatories

The earliest institution for juvenile offenders in Hawai'i was the Industrial and Reformatory School. It was authorized by the legislature in March 1865 and built in Kapālama later that year.

HJH (1980): 98.

Robberies (Train and Bank)

Hawai'i's first—and apparently only—train robbery occurred February 20, 1920, when a masked gunman stopped a slow-moving train of the Kekaha Sugar Company, Ltd., near Mānā, Kaua'i, and escaped with the locomotive and $10,000 taken from the Mānā paymaster on board. Police recovered the loot in a swamp near the home of Kaimiola Hali, a Mānā camp fisherman, whose suspicious behavior soon resulted in his arrest and conviction. Hali, an ardent fan of Western movies, was thought to have been inspired by some of the films he had seen.

Hawai'i's first bank robbery took place at the Pā'ia branch of the Bank of Hawaii on February 3, 1934. Two bandits, one of them armed, took $979.31 from a teller and escaped by automobile. Although neither robber was masked, one sported a large mustache he had painted on himself with an eyebrow pencil. Captured a few hours later, the culprits turned out to be two brothers from Lahaina, David and George Wong.

No other bank robberies were reported until 1955, when the American Security Bank on Beretania Street and the Bank of Hawaii's Pā'ia branch (again) were held up.

HSB, 3 Feb. 1934, 1; HSB, 5 Feb. 1934, 1; HSB, 7 Feb.1934, 1, 4; HA, 13 July 1960, A1B; Condé and Best (1973): 142–144.

Medicine and Health

Abortion

Abortion—called *ōmilo*, *milo*, or *milomilo* by the Hawaiians—has existed in the Islands since pre-contact times. Early accounts of the practice suffer from imprecise terminology. Nineteenth-century writers often equated abortion with infanticide, a term that means something different to modern readers.

A law classifying infanticide as murder was enacted in 1835. The Penal Code of 1850 forbade abortion as well (except to save the woman's life), under penalty of a fine up to $1,000 or imprisonment at hard labor for up to five years.

The law forbidding abortion remained in effect until March 11, 1970, when Hawai'i became the first state in the union to legitimize abortion on demand.

Pukui and Elbert (1986); Gutmanis (1977): 90; Thurston (1904): 105–106; Penal Code 1850, ch. 12, p. 22; SLH 1970, Act 1; *HJH* (1974): 91, 101.

AIDS

A fifty-year-old Oriental woman had the earliest officially recorded case of AIDS (acquired immune deficiency syndrome) in Hawai'i. She was diagnosed with the disease in May 1978 and died in August of that year.

SHDB 1986: 91.

Ambulances

In February 1916, the Honolulu Police Department put into use an ambulance for emergency hospital work. The ambulance body was built atop a Pierce-Arrow chassis, which had formerly supported a sixty-horsepower, $6,000 passenger car traded in by its owner to Schuman Carriage Company.

The first "real" ambulance, built from the wheels up with the sole purpose of operating as an ambulance, was put into operation in Honolulu in 1928.

PCA, 20 Feb. 1916, Feature sec., 6; *The Queen's Hospital Bulletin*, Nov. 1928.

Anesthesia

On February 16, 1850, Dr. Charles H. Wetmore, the mission physician in Hilo, administered ether to his wife, Lucy, as she was giving birth to their first child. Dr. Wetmore's subsequent account of this delivery appears to be the earliest known reference to the use of general anesthesia in the Islands.

The first documented use of an anesthetic in dental surgery occurred in Hilo on September 26, 1868. An entry in Isabella Lyman's journal for that date states, "Fred and I went to Doctor's [presumably Dr. Wetmore], and he took out a tooth of mine. He used the ether spray and they say I fainted after it."

HMJ, Oct. 1981, 291–292; Isabella Lyman journal, HMCS.

Autopsies

On February 17, 1824, following the death of William Beals in Honolulu, Dr. Law opened the chest of the corpse to determine the nature of the disorder. This autopsy is the first mentioned in the historical record. Dr. Law, a Scotsman, was the king's physician and surgeon.

HMJ, Oct. 1981, 284.

Birth Control

Many birth control techniques have been tried in Hawai'i during the past two centuries. The early Hawaiians placed the leaves of different plants into the vagina as contraceptives. One of the plants used for this technique was the tannin-rich *koa*. The *hau* tree was another contraceptive material. Its bark produced a mucus-like substance that may have been used as a spermicide.

Other birth control methods either existed among the native population or were introduced by nineteenth-century settlers from Europe and America. These included coitus interruptus (withdrawal), rhythm, sponges or tampons placed in the vagina, and douches.

In 1914, the Committee on the Social Evil noted, "Soldiers are encouraged to use prophylatics [sic], which are freely dispensed." Although the specific type of prophylactic was not identified, the writers were presumably referring to condoms.

The appearance of condoms in Hawai'i would surely have occurred by the 1890s and might well have taken place earlier in the century. The first unambiguous published reference to their use in the Islands, however, was in 1937.

Eventually, private hospitals, welfare agencies, and plantations offered counseling and services in contraception and sterilization. The first such services were provided on the plantations in 1929 and were extended during the following decade. In Honolulu, Palama Settlement established a male sterilization clinic in 1930 and a women's birth control clinic in 1931.

The first commercially produced oral contraceptive, Enovid, became available in 1957 for endometriosis and cycle control. Approved two years later by federal authorities for use as a birth control pill, it was marketed for such purposes beginning August 18, 1960. It became available in Hawai'i in 1960 for contraceptive use soon after its national release.

Family planning achieved official acceptance in the mid-1960s. In September 1965, the State Department of Health incorporated genetic counseling, fertility control, and sterility correction into its regular programs. Hawaii Planned Parenthood, Inc., was chartered on August 16, 1966.

Gutmanis (1977): 88–90; *Report of Committee on the Social Evil, Honolulu Social Survey, May 1914* (1914): 11, 13; *Transactions, 47th Annual Meeting, Medical Society of Hawaii, 1937*: 67–68; *Transactions, 42nd Annual Meeting, Medical Society of Hawaii, 1932*: 37; John Williams, Director, Hawaii Planned Parenthood, interviewed by Schmitt, 22 Nov. and 16 Dec. 1976; David Kistler, Searle Pharmaceuticals, Inc., memorandum to Thomas S. Kang, 29 Feb. 1980; William H. Hindle, MD, Straub Hospital, interviewed by Schmitt, 17 Mar. 1980; HJH (1974): 95–97, 100–101, 104–105.

Blood Banks

The origins of the Blood Bank of Hawaii date to the months preceding the Pearl Harbor attack. In December 1940, a blood bank was proposed to the Public Health Committee of the Chamber of Commerce of Honolulu, a group that often provided financial support for innovative public health programs. One of the leading proponents was Dr. Eric Fennel, who is credited with giving the first blood transfusion in Hawai'i in 1921. For several years, he operated his own blood bank by storing blood in the icebox in his home.

The Blood Bank of Hawaii was set up in the City and County Emergency Hospital, and the first blood was drawn on June 2, 1941. Public response was rather tepid, and after five months of operation on a demonstration basis, the bank closed on November 13. On December 7, it was quickly reactivated on a twenty-four-hour basis and put under the Office of Civilian Defense. Outlasting its wartime origin, it remains today an important element of Hawai'i's health care system.

HMJ, Jan. 1942, 204–206; Hodge and Ferris (1950): 47–48.

Dentists

Western dentistry appears to have been introduced to the Islands by members of the Sandwich Islands Mission. As early as 1822, Sybil Bingham wrote in her journal, "Mr. B. has almost daily calls to extract teeth, let blood, administrate medicine, etc."

Hiram Bingham—a minister and not a surgeon or dentist— presumably used a tooth extractor much like the one owned by the Reverend Elias Bond in Kohala after 1841. Bond's instrument, now in the collection of the Mission Houses Museum, is an almost six-inch-long, T-shaped device with a hook at the end of the shaft.

Tooth extractor used by the Rev. Elias Bond in Kohala after 1841. *Drawing by Juliette May Fraser. HHS.*

Newspaper advertisements for toothbrushes and dentifrices began to appear toward mid-century. The earliest was placed by E. Espener in *The Polynesian* on August 29, 1840, announcing, "direct from London . . . Hair and Tooth Brushes." The first mention of tooth powders and pastes came in 1850.

Hawai'i's first professional dentist, Dr. M. B. Stevens, appeared on the local scene in December 1847, advertised his services over a twelve-week period, and then dropped out of sight. The first dentist to settle permanently in Hawai'i was John Mott Smith. Dr. Smith arrived early in 1851 and remained an Island resident until his death forty-four years later, after a distinguished career as a dentist, editor, and government official.

HJH (1983): 143–155.

Doctors

The first Western medical practitioners to visit Hawai'i were the six surgeons and surgeon's mates on the *Resolution* and *Discovery*, the two British ships under the command of Captain James Cook. The ships dropped anchor off Waimea, Kaua'i, on January 20, 1778.

The first Island residents treated by these surgeons were several Hawaiians who came aboard at Maui on November 30, 1778. They complained of venereal disease and were given medication.

Don Francisco de Paula Marin arrived in Hawai'i in 1793 or 1794 and eventually became the first resident physician of record (other than native practitioners, known as *kāhuna lapa'au*). Marin, an Island resident until his death in 1837, apparently lacked any formal medical training.

Juan Elliot d'Castro, formerly a surgeon on naval and merchant vessels and at a Rio de Janeiro hospital, came to Hawai'i about 1811 and served as secretary and physician to Kamehameha I. He was apparently the first trained foreign doctor to reside in the Islands.

Both Sarah E. Pierce, MD, and Frances M. Wetmore, MD, received their licenses from the Kingdom's Board of Health in 1883, becoming Hawai'i's earliest women physicians.

In 1921, Dr. George F. Straub and four other physicians founded The Clinic, Hawai'i's first group practice, at 401 South Beretania Street, Honolulu.

HMJ, Oct. 1981, 284–289; Peterson (1984): 115–117.

Epidemics

Hawai'i's earliest recorded epidemic occurred in 1804, when O'ahu was struck with the *'ōku'u*, now thought to have been Asiatic cholera. The death toll was probably less than 15,000, although later writers reported much higher figures.

HMJ, May-June 1970, 359–364.

Eyeglasses

The first optical devices in Hawai'i came aboard the ships of Captain James Cook in 1778 and 1779. Cook's vessels were equipped with several telescopes and a microscope. Whether Cook or any of his officers, scientists, or crew wore eyeglasses is, however, unknown.

Many foreign ships anchored in Island waters during the ensuing half century, and it seems likely that at least some of their masters or officers used spectacles, if only for reading. The possession of eyeglasses by common seamen seems much less probable, given their high cost—as much as $100 for an ordinary pair in the United States in the late 1700s—and the low shipboard wage levels of the day.

One of the earliest visitors definitely known to wear spectacles was Lieutenant Charles R. Malden, surveyor on the HMS *Blonde* in 1825. The Hawaiians, who gave most of the officers nicknames in their own language, dubbed Malden "the man with four eyes."

The eyeglasses brought from Boston by Mercy Whitney may have been the first actually owned by a Hawai'i resident. Mercy, the wife of Samuel Whitney and a member of the Pioneer Company of missionaries, arrived in Hawai'i in April 1820. After more than a decade, her glasses had apparently reached the end of their useful-

The earliest reference to "opticians" in a Honolulu newspaper advertisement, printed in the Hawaiian Gazette *for September 10, 1879.* HHS.

ness. Late in 1830, she wrote: "The glasses which I purchased before I left home, hurt my head, so that I cannot wear them."

The first Island shop to sell eyeglasses, beginning in 1846, was the Honolulu jewelry store of E. H. Boardman, a watch and chronometer maker.

By 1916, optometry had emerged as a separate discipline in Hawai'i. In that year, the directory presented its first classified listing of optometrists, consisting initially of a single establishment: Wall & Dougherty, "Jewelers, Goldsmiths, Platinumsmiths, Silversmiths, Opticians and Optometrists."

Following a visit to Germany, Dr. Gideon M. Van Poole brought the first contact lenses to the Islands about 1930, but whether any were actually worn in Hawai'i during the next ten to fifteen years is unknown. The first optometrist to specialize in contact lenses was Dr. Kwai Cho Choy, in 1946.

Late in 1969, Dr. Percival H. Y. Chee performed Hawai'i's first intraocular lens implantation.

HJH (1985): 134–148; HJH (1993): 241.

Fetal Surgery

The first surgery performed on a fetus in Hawai'i took place March 24, 1989, at Kapiolani Medical Center for Women and Children. Dr. Robert F. Monoson successfully operated on Lisa-Ann Alvarez and the twenty-nine-week-old baby in her uterus to relieve an obstruction of uterine flow from the baby's kidney to its bladder.

HA, 25 Mar. 1989, A2; HSB, 25 Mar. 1989, A1; SSB&A, 26 Mar. 1989, A3.

Hospitals

Hawai'i's first hospital was a small convalescent facility operated by Anthony D. Allen on his property near the present intersection of Punahou and King Streets. During the 1820s, ill or injured seamen and sea captains were taken there to recuperate.

The Queen's Hospital's first permanent structure, erected in 1860. AH.

The first hospital for foreign sailors, the British Hospital for Seamen, was established about 1833. It actually consisted of board in a "hovel" owned by an English tavernkeeper. In 1837, the first real hospital, the Hospital for American Seamen, was established in rented quarters in Waikīkī.

Dr. S. Porter Ford and Dr. George A. Lathrop opened the first private hospital in May 1852 in Nuʻuanu Valley. The Queen's Hospital was established in temporary quarters in 1859, and in December 1860 moved to its permanent 124-bed structure—the first major hospital in the Islands.

In 1907, Tripler Hospital, the first military hospital in Hawaiʻi, was built in Moanalua.

HMJ, July-Aug. 1949, 424–427; HMJ, Mar.-Apr. 1956, 338–341; Kuykendall (1953): 73–74; HJH (1992): 71; HJH (1993): 240.

Opened in Kapālama in 1866, the Oahu Insane Asylum served long-term psychiatric patients. AH.

Insane Asylums

In 1862, the Hawai'i legislature voted to establish an insane asylum. Four years later, the first patients were moved into a newly opened asylum at Kapālama.

SLH 1862: 31–32; HG, 25 Aug. 1866, 3; HG, 6 Oct. 1866, 2.

Leprosy (Hansen's Disease)

In 1845, Dr. Dwight Baldwin treated a high chief who apparently had leprosy or Hansen's disease. The high chief had caught the disease some five years earlier. This seems to have been the earliest recorded case of leprosy, although it was not recognized at the time.

Halford (1954): 215–216.

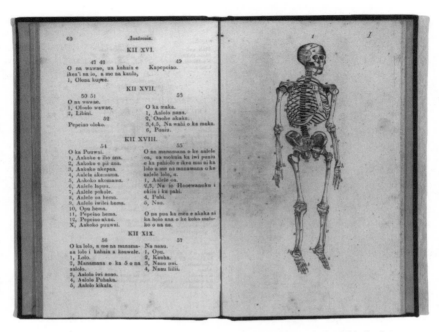

A page from Anatomia *("Anatomy"), the first medical work published in Hawai'i.* HHS.

Medical Books

In 1838, the Lahainaluna Press issued the first medical work ever printed in the Hawaiian language. Dr. Gerrit P. Judd's sixty-page *Anatomia* was illustrated with nineteen copper plates containing fifty-eight engravings.

Halford (1954): 159, 290.

Medical Schools

On November 9, 1870, Dr. Gerrit P. Judd started Hawai'i's first medical school, for Hawaiian students only, with funds provided by the 1868 and 1870 legislatures. The student body numbered ten.

The class completed its work in October 1872, and, after Dr. Judd died, the school closed.

In July 1962, the Department of Public Health was established in the Graduate School of the University of Hawai'i. The department became the School of Public Health in September 1965. A School of Medicine was also created at the University of Hawai'i in that year.

HHR, *Selected Readings* (1969): 107–121; HMJ, Oct. 1981, 285, 288.

Medical Societies

On July 19, 1856, a charter was granted to the Hawaiian Medical Society, the first such organization in the Islands. At the first meeting, held August 13, members elected Dr. R. W. Wood president.

HMJ, Mar.-Apr. 1956, 313.

Medicare

Medicare was instituted in Hawai'i on July 1, 1966. Seventy-one-year-old Tsuri Hirakawa was the first Island resident to be reimbursed under the medical care portion of the program.

HSB, 8 July 1966, A2; HSB, 19 July 1966, A9.

Nurses

Seven members of the Third Order of St. Francis, including Mother Marianne Cope, arrived in 1883 to serve as administrators and nurses at Branch Hospital in Honolulu and Malulani Hospital on Maui. In 1886, the Queen's Hospital hired the first professional nurse, Mary Adams, but her duties were largely those of a matron.

Three years later, in 1889, the Queen's Hospital reportedly employed its first trained nurse, variously identified as Mrs. Johnston,

Mrs. Miller, or left unnamed. The first graduate trained nurses, Margaret A. Carroll and Nina Cook, were hired by the Queen's Hospital in 1892. In 1906, Palama Settlement provided the first public health nurse in the Islands.

The Queen's Hospital School of Nursing, established in 1916, became the first accredited nursing school in Hawai'i five years later. A new law in 1917 established a board of registration of nurses and created the title of registered nurse for those passing an examination.

The University of Hawai'i Nursing School enrolled its first students in September 1952.

HMJ, Oct. 1981, 286–287; Peterson (1984): 90–93.

Open-Heart Surgery

On December 2, 1959, a surgical-technical team of fourteen at the Queen's Hospital performed the first open-heart surgery in the Islands. The patient was Harumi Yoshimoto of Hilo.

HA, 3 Dec. 1959, A1; HA, 4 Dec. 1959, A8.

Opium

Early settlers from China introduced opium smoking to the Islands. Tyhune, a Chinese businessman in Honolulu from 1833 to 1853, provided rooms for addicts from his country.

Dr. Dwight Baldwin and other mission physicians frequently used opium in the form of laudanum to treat their patients. All of the opium seems to have been imported.

Report of Special Committee on Opium to the Legislature of 1892: 16; Kuykendall (1967): 301; Daws (1968): 245; Glick (1980): 146; Baldwin Medical Journal, 1836 to 1843 (manuscript, HMCS), entries for 21 Feb. 1836 and 23 Sept. 1837.

Penicillin

Penicillin reached Hawai'i in 1943 but was initially restricted to military use. Beginning in July, the Aiea Naval Hospital used the new drug for the treatment of gonorrhea.

In October 1943, officials decided to undertake the production of penicillin locally at the HSPA Experiment Station on Ke'eaumoku Street. By the end of the year, significant quantities were being produced.

Penicillin was first made available for civilian use in 1944, with the Queen's Hospital designated as the distributing center.

HMJ, Oct. 1981, 287.

Pharmacies

In 1847, three public pharmacies—apparently Hawai'i's first—opened in Honolulu. From January 2 to April 10, Dr. G. Watson advertised his professional services and his office, "where may be found a general assortment of Drugs and Medicines, Perfumes, Fancy Soaps, &c."

On July 1, the clerk of the Home Office wrote to Dr. Robert W. Wood to state that Wood was keeping "a place of business for the Retail Vending of Drugs, Medicines, Perfumery &c of foreign production & manufacture" and hence required a business license. Five days later, a similar letter was sent to Dr. G. W. Hunter.

HMJ, Oct. 1981, 284–285.

Psychiatrists

Dr. Robert B. Faus, a physician for the City and County of Honolulu, began to treat psychiatric patients on an outpatient basis in 1922.

In 1926, Dr. Mon Fah Chung, a neurologist, returned to Honolulu. He offered private psychiatric treatment in addition to his practice of neurology.

Although Dr. Chung appears to have been Hawai'i's first psychiatrist in private practice, he did not list himself in the telephone directory under this specialty until 1953. This was eight years after the first such listing, by Dr. Richard D. Kepner.

HMJ, Oct. 1981, 287.

Pure Food and Drug Laws

Laws prohibiting the adulteration of food and drugs and providing for their inspection were first enacted in Hawai'i in 1903, three years before the passage of the U.S. Pure Food and Drug Act and Meat Inspection Act. The 1903 acts were further strengthened by the territorial legislature in 1911 and 1915, with amendments banning the mislabeling of such products and all false advertising.

SLH 1903, Acts 31 and 50; SLH 1911, Act 77; SLH 1915, Acts 78 and 124.

Quadruplets

Hawai'i's first quadruplets apparently were four Caucasian girls born April 12, 1930, at a camp on the McBryde Plantation in 'Ele'ele, Kaua'i. They weighed between one and two pounds each; two lived several hours, and the other two died the following day.

The first Hawai'i-born quadruplets to survive were born in Tripler Hospital on March 13, 1980. The mother, a Navy wife who had been taking fertility pills, had come to Honolulu from Misawa, Japan, where her husband was stationed, to take advantage of Tripler's obstetric facilities.

No record of quintuplets or higher-order births in Hawai'i can be found.

HSB, 16 Apr. 1930, 3; *HA*, 16 June 1931, 7; *Annual Report, Board of Health, 1930*, 4; *HSB*, 14 Mar. 1980, A2; *HSB*, 15 Mar. 1980, A2; *HA*, 14 Mar. 1980, A1; *SHDB 1987*: 78.

Test-Tube Babies

Hawai'i's first test-tube baby was Jacquelyn Mii Low, born at Kapiolani Women's and Children's Medical Center on December 20, 1985. She was born to Janice and James Low through an in-vitro fertilization procedure.

The Islands' first frozen embryo test-tube baby was Garrett John Costello, born at Kaiser Hospital to Debbie and Bill Costello on December 29, 1991. Conceived in a petri dish sixteen months earlier, Garrett spent his first seven months in cold storage.

HSB, 22 Dec. 1986, A1, A3; HSB, 3 Jan. 1992, B1, B4.

Tranquilizers

In 1955, psychiatrists at Territorial Hospital began using tranquilizing drugs in the treatment of their patients, often in conjunction with group psychotherapy techniques. The first modern tranquilizer used at the hospital was Chlorpromazine.

HMJ, Oct. 1981, 287.

Transplants and Replants

Led by surgeon Livingston Wong and urologist Herbert Chinn, doctors performed Hawai'i's first successful transplant of a human kidney on August 10, 1969, at St. Francis Hospital in Honolulu. Although the first procedure ended in rejection, the second and third procedures, which took place a few days later, did not.

On December 23, 1977, Dr. James Doyle successfully replanted the severed thumb of Roy Campos, Jr., a Kapa'a rodeo rider, who had lost it while roping a steer at Keālia, Kaua'i. Although replants had been tried previously in Hawai'i, this one, performed at the Queen's Medical Center, was the first successful effort.

Eleven-year-old Don Torres, who had aplastic anemia, received Hawai'i's first bone marrow transplant on March 31, 1978.

Livingston Wong also headed this transplant team at St. Francis Hospital.

Hawai'i's first successful heart transplant took place on March 10 and 11, 1987, when fifty-year-old Glen B. Silva received the heart of sixteen-year-old Michael R. Benson, a traffic accident victim. The four-hour operation was performed at St. Francis Hospital by Dr. Ricardo Moreno and a twenty-two-person transplant team.

Joan Yoder received the state's first successful liver transplant at St. Francis Medical Center on May 17 and 18, 1993. Dr. Linda Wong led the team of surgeons and nurses. By that time, St. Francis had performed more than 400 kidney transplants, eighty bone marrow transplants, and twenty heart transplants.

Hawai'i's first combined pancreas and kidney transplant recipient was Mary Sentinella. Performed at St. Francis Medical Center June 28, 1993, the seven-hour operation was the state's first-ever pancreas transplant and also the first combined liver and pancreas transplant.

HMJ, Oct. 1981, 288; HSB, 11 Mar. 1987, A1; HSB, 12 Mar. 1987, A1, A6; HMJ, Apr. 1988, 177–181; HA, 7 Mar. 1988, A1; HA, 21 May 1993, D4; HA, 9 June 1993, A3; HA, 7 July 1993, A6; HA, 16 July 1993, A9.

Vaccinations

Some time during his stay in the Islands from 1823 to 1826, Dr. Abraham Blatchley obtained a supply of cowpox vaccine from London by way of Nantucket, Massachusetts. By the time he received the shipment, however, it was too old and no longer effective.

In 1839, following a smallpox scare, 8,000 to 10,000 Hawaiians were vaccinated in Honolulu in Hawai'i's first mass immunization effort.

More than a century later, two months after the Pearl Harbor attack, Hawai'i's military government instituted another mass immunization, this time against both smallpox and typhoid fever. As reported by the *Hawaii Health Messenger*, "This was the first time mass immunization against typhoid fever and small pox was required of the entire population of a state or territory. It was also the first time the vaccination status of the entire population of a state or territory was recorded."

HMJ, Oct. 1981, 284; Hawaii State Department of Health, *Hawaii Health Messenger*, Winter 1991, 1–2.

Veterinarians

Although animal diseases and injuries were undoubtedly treated early in the nineteenth century, no references to professional veterinarians have been found before the 1880s. The earliest is an 1882 law establishing quarantine stations and authorizing the appointment of "competent persons as Inspectors of Animals" at each port.

The 1884 census—the first to include a category for "veterinary surgeons"— reported two such persons in the Kingdom: presumably A. T. Baker of Honolulu and Dr. James Brodie, who was appointed later that year as government veterinarian on Maui.

SLH 1882, ch. 34; *Census of the Hawaiian Islands . . . 1884*; *McKenney's Hawaiian Directory [1884–1885]*: 97; Interior Department, Book 25, p. 227, 24 Oct. 1884, AH.

X-Rays

On September 8, 1896, Dr. Lauschner, acting surgeon of the SS *Australia*, gave the first Island demonstration of the X-ray. Speaking before some seventy-five invited guests in Pauahi Hall, Punahou, Dr. Lauschner exhibited X-ray plates he had made and projected first his hand and then a coin-filled purse on a fluoroscopic screen.

The Honolulu Sanitarium, at 1082 South King Street, reported in 1899 that "a fine Satic [static] electrical machine, with an X-ray attachment, is in operation, and is for the use of physicians, and for giving special electrical treatment." This appears to be the earliest reference to the use of the X-ray in an Island institution.

Hawai'i's first whole body computerized tomography (CT) scanner was installed at St. Francis Hospital in May 1978, and the first patient was scanned later that month.

In 1986, Hawaii Health Technologies set up the state's first magnetic resonance imager (MRI), in partnership with five Oʻahu hospitals, at the MRI Center of the Pacific at Kewalo Basin.

HMJ, Oct. 1981, 286, 288; HA, 13 May 1982, C1; HA, 14 May 1982, A6; HA, 18 Aug. 1990, A1, A4.

Religion

Bibles

The earliest Hawaiian translation from Holy Scripture was a leaflet containing the 100th psalm, distributed at the dedication of Kawaiahao Church on November 19, 1825.

The first Hawaiian edition of the New Testament was completed in 1832, and the entire Bible—*Ka Palapala Hemolele*, in three volumes and 2,331 duodecimo pages—was in print by May 10, 1839.

HJH (1979): 109.

Punchbowl Sunrise Prayer Services

Sunrise prayer services on Punchbowl are now an Easter morning tradition in Honolulu. The earliest occurred April 15, 1906.

HS, 11 Apr. 1906, 5.

Religions

Religion first appeared in Hawai'i in ancient times. A number of gods were worshiped by both ali'i and commoners. An organized priesthood conducted services for the ali'i. Public services, sometimes lasting several days, were held at *heiau* (places of worship).

The ancient Hawaiian form of religion collapsed in 1819, when Queen Keopuolani, mother of King Liholiho, ate with her son Kauikeaouli and broke the *kapu*. Soon afterward, the *heiau* and their temple images were destroyed.

Arriving from Boston in 1820, Protestant missionaries quickly established themselves in Honolulu and elsewhere in the Kingdom. After more than a year of conducting services in their living quarters and various outdoor locations, they erected the first church edifice in the Islands, a small thatched structure. This church, the original Kawaiahao Church, was later replaced by a succession of thatched churches, culminating in the present coral stone building, dedicated on July 21, 1842. The first stone church in Hawai'i was Wainee, built at Lahaina in 1828.

The first Roman Catholic missionaries arrived in Honolulu on July 7, 1827, from Bordeaux, France. Led by Father Alexis Bachelot, they held the first mass of record on Hawaiian soil on July 14, 1827. For the remainder of the year, one of the three grass huts on the parcel rented by the mission was used as a chapel. In January 1828, they completed a new structure, half of which, seating forty persons, was set aside as a chapel.

Initially persecuted and on two occasions expelled, the Catholic mission finally won official toleration in 1839. A year later, ground was broken for the Cathedral of Our Lady of Peace. Blessed and dedicated on August 15, 1843, this cathedral still stands on Fort Street.

The first Mormon missionaries arrived in Honolulu from San Francisco in December 1850. The Hawaiian branch of the Church of Jesus Christ of Latter-day Saints was established at Kealakou, Maui, on August 8, 1851. The Mormon Temple, built at Lā'ie in 1919, was the first to be built outside of Salt Lake City.

The Anglican Church was not formally established in the Islands until 1862, but its history in Hawai'i dates back to Captain James Cook's visit. In January 1779, the first Christian service on Hawaiian soil was conducted at Nāpō'opo'o, at the burial of a member of Cook's crew. The Book of Common Prayer of the Church of England was used for the service. Hawai'i's first resident clergyman was John Howel, an Anglican minister who spent about a year at Kealakekua in 1794 and 1795.

Although Hawai'i has had a small Jewish population for well over a century, no formal religious organization existed until the creation of the Jewish Welfare Board in Honolulu immediately after World War I. Later, during World War II, a Jewish center was established on Young Street. Temple Emanu-El was chartered in 1950, and a permanent temple was built on Pali Highway and dedicated in 1960.

Chinese religion, as practiced in Hawai'i, is a mixture of Buddhism, Taoism, and Confucianism. Most of the temples are family owned and family administered. These family shrines have probably existed from the days of the first Chinese arrivals in Hawai'i.

Buddhism grew rapidly following the influx of Japanese plantation laborers after 1885. In April 1889, a small, temporary church was built on Emma Street, marking the beginnings of the Honpa Hongwanji Mission of Hawaii.

In 1982, a survey by the Department of Religion of the University of Hawai'i counted eighty-three denominations in the state: twenty-one Buddhist, twenty-eight Protestant, six other Christian (including Roman Catholic, by far the leading church in membership), nine Indian or Hindu, two Jewish, one Muslim, seven new religious movements of Japanese origin, five Shinto, and four other faiths.

Feher, Joesting, and Bushnell (1969): 100–101, 172, 186, 188–189; Mulholland (1970): 19, 48–49, 92, 94–97, 117–118, 141, 143–144, 150, 243–245, 254, 277, 296; Bingham (1849): 133; Historic Buildings Task Force (1969): buildings 28, 41, 81; [Hiram Bingham,] *Early Hawaiian Churches and Their Manner of Building* (Honolulu: 1924): 23; Yzendoorn (1927): 33, 35, 51, 151; *All About Hawaii/HAA 1956*: 142–143, 146, 150–157; *32nd Annual Report, HHS, 1923*: 54–60; SHDB 1986: 58–59.

Amusements and Diversions

Almanacs

The earliest Hawaiian almanac, *Alemanaka Hawaii, No Ka Makahiki o ko Kakou Haku o Iesu Kristo 1835* (Hawaiian Almanac, for the year of our Lord Jesus Christ 1835), was published at the Mission Press in 1834. It included astronomical data for the sun, moon, and planets; the hours of sunrise, sunset, moonrise, and moonset; and important events in Island history.

Anon. (1834); Judd, Bell, and Murdoch (1978): 35–36.

Aquariums

The Waikiki Aquarium, in Kapiʻolani Park, formally opened

The Waikiki Aquarium was created in 1904 as an attraction at the end of the Waikīkī streetcar line. UH.

March 19, 1904. Although initially built and operated by the Honolulu Rapid Transit and Land Company, the City and County of Honolulu assumed control in July 1919. The aquarium is currently operated by the University of Hawai'i.

F, Apr. 1904, 19; *HAA* 1904: 217–220; *Annual Report of the Honolulu Rapid Transit and Land Co.* for 1904 (p. 15) and 1919 (p. 9).

Automobile Floral Parades

Honolulu's first motor car fiesta was held on Thanksgiving Day, 1904. Eighteen or nineteen automobiles, all decorated with flowers, paraded from Iolani Palace to Kapi'olani Park, then returned by way of Makiki to Union Square. Captain Robert Graham won first prize with a Japanese motif.

The 1904 parade was so successful that another, involving automobiles, carriages, horses, and countless flowers, was held on Washington's Birthday, 1906.

HS, 23 Nov. 1904, 6; HS, 25 Nov. 1904, 7; *PP*, Dec. 1904, 15; *PP*, Apr. 1906, 12–37.

Beauty Contests

The Ka Palapala Beauty Pageant, the first full-scale beauty contest in the Islands in 1937, was held annually on the University of Hawaii's Manoa campus for many years. Entrants represented the major ethnic groups in Hawai'i.

(Lei Day queens had been selected as early as 1928, but these events, strictly speaking, could not be called beauty contests.)

The first Miss Hawaii contest was held May 8, 1948, in connection with the Forty-Ninth State Fair. Irmgard Waiwaiole, a twenty-year-old hapa-haole brunette, won the title. In July, however, she abdicated her crown, unable to complete the necessary high school credits in time for the September 1 Miss America deadline. She was replaced by Yun Tau Zane, a University of Hawai'i coed who became Hawai'i's first representative in the Miss America contest.

Debbye Turner, the first Hawai'i-born Miss America, was crowned in 1989. Turner was born in 1965 at Schofield Barracks, where her father was serving in the Army. After four or five years, she and her parents moved to the mainland, and she entered the Atlantic City competition as Miss Missouri.

The first Hawai'i resident to be crowned

Carolyn Sapp was a junior at Hawaii Pacific University when, in 1991, she became the first Hawai'i resident to be crowned Miss America. HPU.

Miss America was Carolyn Suzanne Sapp, on September 14, 1991. Born in Washington State in 1967, she moved to Hawai'i in 1985 and was a junior at Hawaii Pacific University when she won the Miss Hawaii and Miss America titles.

Kobayashi (1983): 60; *HA*, 7 Mar. 1948, 14; *HA*, 9 May 1948, 1; *HA*, 13 May 1948, 4; *HSB*, 1 Sept. 1948, 3; *HSB*, 2 Sept. 1948, 10; *HA*, mag. sec., 19 Apr. 1953, 6–7; *HSB*, 19 Sept. 1989, A1; *SSB&A*, 15 Sept. 1991, A1, A8.

Board Games

Hawai'i's first board game was *kōnane*. Archibald Campbell, an O'ahu resident from 1809 to 1810, described it as "a game somewhat resembling draughts [checkers], but more complicated. It is played upon a board about twenty-two by fourteen, painted black, with white spots, on which the men are placed . . . the game is won by the capture of the adversary's pieces. Tamaahmaah excels at this game. I have seen him sit for hours playing with his chiefs."

Checkers apparently arrived in the Islands in 1791, when Captain John Kendrick of the *Lady Washington*, gave a set to Kaahumanu. The game soon became popular, and the Hawaiians learned to play it well.

Chess was probably played in Hawai'i—at least by some haole residents or visiting ships' officers—by the 1830s. The earliest chess club, the Steinitz Chess Club, was organized in March 1890. Members paid a five-dollar entrance fee and one-dollar monthly dues and met in rooms on Alakea Street. Beset by low membership, they voted to disband in August 1891, less than seventeen months after their first meeting.

Campbell (1967): 147; Silverman (1987): 52; *PCA*, 18 Mar. 1890, 3; *PCA*, 26 Mar. 1890, 3; *PCA*, 28 Mar. 1890, 3; *PCA*, 7 Aug. 1891, 3.

Books

The first book published in the Islands was a sixty-page hymnal, *Na Himeni Hawaii*, prepared by William Ellis and Hiram

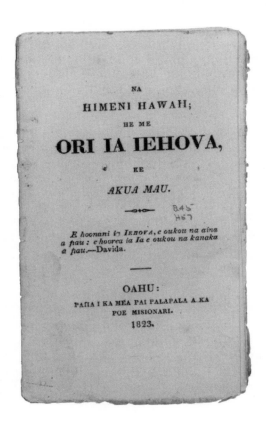

This 60-page hymnal, issued in 1823, was the earliest book published by the Mission Press. HHS.

Bingham. Issued in October 1823, it contained the lyrics to forty-seven songs, many of them original.

The earliest illustrated book, *He Ninau Hoike no ka mooolelo o ka Palapala Hemolele* (A historical catechism of the Holy Scriptures), included three simple woodcuts by Bingham that depicted Noah's Ark, the Tower of Babel, and Sodom and Gomorrah. Although dated 1830, this book was not completed until March 1831.

Day and Loomis (1973): 12; Forbes (1992b): 52.

Bowling Alleys

Bowling alleys were introduced to Hawai'i soon after the beginning of the whaling era. During the 1820s, the foreign population rolled tenpins at Anthony Allen's tavern. In 1837, the Hotel Waititi advertised "a Bowling Alley and such other facilities for amusement and recreation" and later boasted of its "spacious adobie built rolling alley."

For a brief period in 1843, Herman Melville (who later wrote *Moby Dick*) worked as a pinsetter in a Honolulu "ball alley."

Viewed as something of a public nuisance, bowling alleys eventually fell from favor. A renewal of interest occurred around 1917, but it was not until 1937 that the first modern bowling establishment opened, the ten-lane Pla-Mor at Hotel and Richards Streets.

HJH (1980): 82.

Bungee Jumping

Bungee jumping was introduced to Hawai'i at the Fiftieth State Fair on the Aloha Stadium grounds, May 28, 1993. The cost was sixty-nine dollars per jump from the 130-foot-high arch erected at the site.

HA, 29 May 1993, A1, A2.

Burlesque

The Islands' pioneer burlesque house, the Beretania Theatre, was located at 1229 Kamanuwai Lane in a congested urban slum a block mauka of Chinatown. Built around 1936 or 1937 as a neighborhood movie theater, the Beretania was bought in 1944 by William C. Ferreira and used thereafter mostly for adults-only films. Three years later, Ferreira renamed his theater the Beretania Follies, erected a saucy neon sign above its entrance, and initiated regular stage shows, beginning in July 1947 with "Cover Girl Scandals."

Most of the strippers appearing at Island theaters and night clubs in the years that followed were from the mainland and overseas, but in 1959 a local girl achieved stripping stardom. Billed as "Orchid Kainoa," Jeanette Morse performed at the Ginbasha and other Honolulu night spots during the era.

Polk's Directory of City and County of Honolulu for 1936–1937 (p. 809), 1937–1938 (p. 98), 1941–1942 (p. 103), and 1947–1948 (p. 102); *HSB*, 26 Apr. 1967, C16; advertisements in *HSB*, 27 June 1945 (p. 8), 30 Sept. 1945 (p. 8), 1 July 1947 (p. 12), 5 July 1947 (p. 19), 2 Sept. 1947 (p. 8). For a picture of Orchid Kainoa, see Ginbasha ad in *HSB*, 3 Dec. 1959, 32. The dancer's legal name was provided by Nathan Napoka, whose stepfather, Jack O'Brien, was active in the entertainment industry at that time.

Card Games

Foreign seamen introduced card games to Hawai'i during the 1790s and early 1800s. During the reign of Kamehameha I, the Hawaiians in Honolulu, who were great gamblers, quickly learned the new games and became very skillful.

Card playing was especially popular among the members of royalty. Agents of the Hudson's Bay Company, visiting the king and Liholiho in Kailua in 1816, taught the latter how to play whist, a game that soon became popular. The only card game the people and chiefs had known before then was the already-known game called "Nuuanu."

Daws (1966): 44; Ii (1983): 127.

Cockfighting

Cockfighting, or *ho'ohākā moa*, was a popular sport with the ali'i in ancient Hawai'i and involved heavy betting.

Declared a misdemeanor in 1884 in legislation outlawing cruelty to animals, cockfighting lost much of its earlier popularity by the end of the nineteenth century. Following the influx of Filipino plantation workers after 1906, however, it quickly regained its place as a major, although illegal, spectator sport.

Malo (1951): 230–231; SLH 1884, chap. LI, sec. 2; *All About Hawaii*, vol. 90 (1968): 25–27; Takaki (1983): 53; HSB, 2 Feb. 1944, 3; series by Elma Y. Cabral in HSB, 18–22 Mar. 1949.

Comic Strips

The earliest comic strips carried in an Island newspaper appeared in the *Evening Bulletin* beginning on January 30, 1904. Seven multi-panel strips, all in color, formed a weekly comic supplement. The cartoons apparently failed to attract much of a readership, and the feature was eventually dropped.

The first daily comic strip in a Honolulu newspaper was Bud Fisher's "Mutt and Jeff," which made its *Star-Bulletin* debut on March 7, 1916. *The Advertiser* avoided comic strips until April 16, 1920, when, with obvious misgivings, it began daily publication of George McManus' "Bringing Up Father."

HJH (1978): 109; HJH (1993): 239–240.

Crossword Puzzles

Hawai'i's earliest crossword puzzles appeared in the *Star-Bulletin* on November 6, 1924, and in *The Advertiser* on January 12, 1925.

HJH (1978): 109.

Dictionaries

Published at Lahainaluna, Maui, in 1836, Lorrin Andrews' 5,700-word *Vocabulary of Words in the Hawaiian Language* was the earliest full-scale Hawaiian dictionary.

A number of shorter word lists appeared before Andrews' *Vocabulary*. The first, a 250-word collection by William Anderson, a surgeon on the *Resolution*, was included in Captain James Cook's *Voyage to the Pacific Ocean* (London, 1784).

The earliest English-Hawaiian dictionary published in Hawai'i was *He Hoakakaolelo no na Huaolelo Beritania* (A dictionary of English words), edited by John S. Emerson and Artemas Bishop in 1845.

62nd Annual Report, HHS, 1953: 5–18; Forbes (1992b): 63.

Fiction

The first piece of fiction to use Hawai'i as a setting was E. T. A. Hoffmann's "Haimatochare." This short story was written and printed in German in 1819.

James Jackson Jarves, a former editor of *The Polynesian* newspaper, wrote the first novel with a Hawaiian setting, *Kiana: A Tradition of Hawaii*, in 1857.

HJH (1978): 1–27; Day (1984): 57.

Film Festivals

The first Hawaii International Film Festival, held November 1–7, 1981, featured seven films from six countries. Five thousand viewers attended the screenings at the Varsity Theatre.

HA, 18 July 1981, B3; SSB&A, 1 Nov. 1981, C11; HA, 14 Nov. 1989, supp.

Fireworks

Captain James Cook, who previously entertained the Tongans and Society Islanders with fireworks displays, had largely depleted his supply by the time he reached Hawai'i. Even so, following a boxing match at Kealakekua Bay on February 2, 1779, he set off a few water rockets and two sky rockets before a group of astonished natives. This exhibition of Western pyrotechnics was not repeated until March 1792, when Captain George Vancouver set off fireworks at Waimea, Kaua'i. A third display, also provided by Vancouver, took place at Kealakekua twenty-three months later.

The earliest effort to regulate fireworks appeared in the Penal Code of 1850, which described their firing as a "common nuisance" and required would-be users to obtain a permit.

Beaglehole (1967), part two: 1174; 69th Annual Report, HHS, 1960: 7; SSB&A, 16 Mar. 1980, A1, A4.

First Night

Honolulu's first First Night, a non-alcoholic New Year's Eve celebration, took place December 31, 1990. Organizers estimated that about 50,000 people walked around downtown to see eighty-seven artists and entertainers stationed at thirty-seven sites from Chinatown to Thomas Square.

First Night was funded through grants, corporate sponsorships, and the sale of First Night buttons, which cost five dollars. The buttons admitted the wearer to various indoor performances.

HA, 28 Dec. 1990, C1, C2; HA, 1 Jan. 1991, A3; HA, 2 Jan. 1991.

Guidebooks

The earliest Hawaiian guidebook aimed at visitors and potential visitors was Henry M. Whitney's *Hawaiian Guide Book*, first published by the author in 1875 and later issued in revised editions.

Although Hawai'i had been described in numerous earlier works, some dating from the late eighteenth century, none was written for tourist use. These predecessor publications included accounts of voyages, personal reminiscences, travelers' impressions, and political or economic descriptions.

Whitney (1875); Whitney (1890).

Lei Day

Lei Day was first observed on May 1, 1928. The holiday had been proposed by Don Blanding, an artist and writer then working in the advertising department of the *Honolulu Star-Bulletin*.

Grace Tower Warren, the newspaper's society editor, liked the idea and recommended that May Day, traditionally associated with thoughts of love and flowers, be set aside as Lei Day in Hawai'i. That day also happened to be her birthday. Blanding promoted the May Day–Lei Day combination and gained support from the business community.

The first Lei Day entertainment and presentations took place in the lobby of the Bank of Hawaii, at King and Bishop Streets in downtown Honolulu. There was also an exhibit of leis, and the bank provided cash prizes for the winners in several lei-making categories. Nina Bowman, a nineteen-year-old University of Hawai'i student, was selected the Lei Day Queen.

HAA 1929: 104; Blanding (1930): 270–277; HSB, 30 Apr. 1957, 19; HSB, 14 Aug. 1962, sec. 1, p. 13; HSB, 27 Apr. 1968, A12; HA, 30 Apr. 1979, B1.

Libraries

The earliest libraries in Hawai'i were reading rooms provided for ship officers and crews. In Lahaina, the Seamen's Chapel and Reading Room was built in 1834 following an appeal by William Richards and Ephriam Spaulding.

In Honolulu, the Sandwich Islands Institute, organized in November 1837, set up a room at the Seaman's Bethel as a library and a museum of natural history and Pacific artifacts. A newspaper article in October

The Honolulu Library and Reading-Room Association on Alakea Street offered library service from 1879 to 1912. AH.

Interior of the Honolulu Library & Reading Room. HHS.

1840 referred to this as a "Public Library, three to four hundred volumes."

The first true public library in the Islands was the Library of Hawaii, now the Hawaii State Library. It was authorized and funded by the 1909 territorial legislature and opened on February 1, 1913.

HJH (1978), 100.

Magic Lantern Shows

Lord Byron of the HBM *Blonde* presented the earliest known magic lantern show—a precursor of the photographic slide show and film strip—at the home of Billy Pitt (Kalaimoku) on May 28, 1825.

HJH (1978): 102.

Milk Caps

Milk caps have been in use in Hawai'i at least since 1902, when they were produced by Lahainaluna Dairy. The last functional milk bottle was manufactured in 1961 by L&L Dairy, after which milk cartons came into general use in the Islands.

Games involving milk caps date back even further. One such game was reportedly brought to Hawai'i at the turn of the century by early Japanese contract workers.

In the early 1970s, Haleakala Dairy began printing milk caps for game use, mainly on Maui. In 1989, it brought the milk caps to O'ahu to help promote its new passion-orange-guava (POG) drink. The resulting craze is probably attributable to a Waialua Elementary guidance teacher, Blossom Galbiso, who introduced the game into O'ahu schoolyards in 1992.

By early 1993, the manufacture, selling, collecting, and trading of milk caps, along with their use in simple games, had reached epidemic proportions in Hawai'i.

Unofficial Milk Cap Handbook (Honolulu: Liliuokalani School, 1993): 6–7; *H*, June 1993, 10; *HA*, 12 Apr. 1993, B1; *HA*, 30 May 1993, A7; *SSB&A*, 21 Feb. 1993, F1, F8.

Motion Pictures

The earliest motion pictures to be shown in Hawai'i were seven brief scenes screened by Edison's Veriscope at the Opera House on February 5, 1897. The scenes included A *Watermelon Contest*, *Arrival of the Empire State Express*, *The Great McKinley Parade*, and *New York Fire Department on Active Duty*.

On June 10, 1898, while in transit through Honolulu, two Edison photographers, W. Bleckyrden and James White, made the first movies actually filmed in Hawai'i. None of the three scenes— *Honolulu Street Scene*, *Kanakas Diving for Money* (two parts), and *Wharf Scene, Honolulu*—exceeded one minute in screen time.

The first motion picture theater in Hawai'i was Joel C. Cohen's Orpheum, a 945-seat house at 1234 Fort Street. Although films were shown there beginning in 1906, Sunday performances remained forbidden until 1915.

The first Hollywood productions made on location in Hawai'i were two single-reel, hand-colored films, *Hawaiian Love* and *The Shark God*, starring Virginia Brissac and filmed on O'ahu in February 1913.

Talking pictures arrived in 1915, but required another fourteen years to become established. The first local showing was at the Bijou on August 5, 1915, by way of Edison's primitive kinetophone process. The regular showing of talkies did not start until July 1929.

Natural-color travelogues of Hawai'i were first shown shortly after World War I. On December 30, 1918, the *New York Times* favorably reviewed *Kilauea—the Hawaiian Volcano*, made by the Prizma Color process.

In 1947, the Consolidated theater chain installed its first candy counters, and in 1949, it opened a 750-car drive-in theater on Kapiolani Boulevard, the first such theater in the Islands.

HJH (1978): 103–104; Schmitt (1988): 4, 19–21, 23.

Museums

The largest museums in Hawai'i today are the Bernice Pauahi Bishop Museum, devoted to the natural history and ethnology of the Pacific, and the Honolulu Academy of Arts. Founded in 1889, the Bishop Museum opened to the public in 1892. The Honolulu Academy of Arts was incorporated in 1922 and opened in 1927.

Earlier museums, with more modest collections and limited life spans, included the Sandwich Islands Institute and the National Museum. Organized in November 1837, the Sandwich Islands Institute used a room at Honolulu's Seaman's Bethel as a library and museum of natural history and Pacific artifacts.

In 1872, the legislature voted "to establish a National Museum of Archaeology, Literature, Botany, Geology, and Natural History of the Hawaiian Islands." The National Museum, located in a room on the second floor of Aliiolani Hale (now the Judiciary Building),

The Bernice P. Bishop Museum, founded in 1889. AH.

194

opened to visitors in 1875, but was closed in 1898 when its collections were transferred to the Bishop Museum.

HJH (1978): 100; HJH (1977): 21–22; P, 17 Oct. 1840, 74; Frost & Frost, AIA, Aliʻiolani Hale, A Century of Growth and Change, 1872–1977 (Hawaii State Dept. of Accounting & General Services, 1977): 53–55, 139; Rose (1980): 1–5.

Parks

The Privy Council records for January 22, 1850, noted approval "for marking out the boundaries of the square on the Plains of Waikiki, to be called by the name of Admiral Thomas." Honolulu's Thomas Square, the Islands' first public park, remained unimproved until 1873, when plans to fence the area and plant trees were announced.

Emma Square has been described as the first "cared-for park" in Honolulu. Kamehameha IV donated land for the park when Emma Street was opened, sometime before 1863, but development did not take place until 1871.

The first park with extensive recreational facilities was Kapiʻolani Park in 1877. Originally a private venture, the park came under the jurisdiction of the Honolulu Park Commission in 1896 and since that time has been one of Oʻahu's most popular spots.

Hawaii National Park, the earliest under federal jurisdiction, was established August 1, 1916, with acreage on both Maui and the island of Hawaiʻi. In July 1961, the two sections were split into separate parks, Hawaii Volcanoes National Park and Haleakalā National Park.

The earliest territorial parks—in fact if not in name—were ʻAkaka Falls, Kōkeʻe, and Waimea Canyon, all of which were developed before World War II. Formal designation of these parks took place in 1952.

HJH (1978): 100–101.

Phonographs and Records

Recorded sound first reached Hawai'i in 1879, when J. W. Kohler arrived in Honolulu, en route from San Francisco to New Zealand, with an Edison phonograph in his possession. He demonstrated the phonograph to Kalakaua's court at Iolani Palace, and to the public at a benefit performance at the Hawaiian Theater.

The earliest known records of "Hawaiian" music were two Edison cylinders issued at the end of the nineteenth century. One was "Honolulu Cake Walk," a banjo solo by Vess L. Ossman, released between late 1898 and February 1900. The other, "My Honolulu Lady," was sung by Dan W. Quinn and dated either May 1899 or April 1901.

Far more authentic, presumably, were two cylinders listed in a 1901 Columbia Records catalog, "Aloha 'Oe" and "Ku'u Pua i Paoakalani."

The first commercial recording by the Honolulu Symphony Orchestra was *Music from the Majestic Islands*, on a twelve-inch LP released in September 1962.

The first Hawai'i-born symphonic composer to be represented on a major record label was Dai-Keong Lee, born in 1915, whose *Prelude and Hula*, composed in 1939, was recorded for Victor in 1942 by the National Symphony Orchestra. Among other works, Lee wrote the score for a successful Broadway musical, *Teahouse of the August Moon* (1953).

The first Islanders with recordings to lead *Billboard* magazine's "Top Ten" charts were two Punahou graduates, Dave Guard and Bob Shane. They joined Nick Reynolds to form the Kingston Trio and recorded "Tom Dooley," a number one record in 1958.

HJH (1978): 106, 116; HJH (1987): 156; Ewen (1982): 408–410; Hall (1948): 757–758; HSB, 17 Jan. 1944, 1, 6; HSB, 17 Apr. 1948, 11; HA, 16 July 1990, B1.

Roller Coasters

Hawai'i's first roller coaster was erected in Central Park, an amusement park at the corner of Beretania and Punchbowl Streets.

In 1885, its inaugural riders, "a committee of the Chamber of Commerce, a delegation from the Hawaiian Carriage Company, a Merchant Street detachment, and members of the press," enjoyed a private preview and pronounced the experience "a decided success." Their fastest roundtrip was timed at seventeen seconds.

DB, 27 Feb. 1885, 3; DB, 28 Feb. 1885, 3; PCA, 28 Feb. 1885, 3.

Scouts

At a meeting held September 5, 1910, the Boys' Work Committee of the Honolulu YMCA initiated the organization of the first Boy Scout troops in Hawai'i. The earliest of these was known as the Rainbow Troop for the numerous nationalities represented.

The first Girl Scout troop was established in 1917.

HS, 6 Sept, 1910, 6; F, Oct. 1910, 6; F, May 1913, 109–110; Girl Scout Council of the Pacific, Inc., records.

Slot Machines

Hawai'i saw its first slot machine in September 1894, an event marked by the following news item in *The Advertiser*.

"A few weeks ago . . . one of the late inventions in this line was put in use at Merchants' Exchange saloon. This machine gained rapidly in favor. The idea was a simple one. All you had to do was to put a nickel in the slot, and if you were lucky you would get a number of nickels back. But generally you weren't lucky, as the machines were made for business, and not philanthropy."

The police soon closed down this operation.

PCA, 20 Sept. 1894, 7.

Swimming Pools

The first full-scale swimming pools in the Islands were constructed at Punahou School and Kamehameha School for Boys in the late 1880s.

Completed in 1888, Punahou's tank was forty-seven feet long. The Kamehameha School for Boys acquired its pool sometime between October 1887, when the school opened, and 1889, when Uldrick Thompson recorded the existence of a twelve- by eighteen-foot swimming tank.

The earliest swimming pool at an Island hotel appears to have been at the Haleiwa Hotel, opened in Waialua in 1899. Guests praised its "big cemented pool of soft fresh water, filled from the wonderful springs on the old Emerson homestead." The site also offered ocean and river bathing.

In Honolulu, hotels with swimming tanks included the Pleasanton by 1909 and the Colonial by 1915.

The first neighbor island hotel to offer a pool was the Kona Inn at Kailua on the island of Hawai'i. It installed its swimming pool in November 1929.

Home swimming pools were introduced late in the nineteenth century but remained relatively rare until the post-World War II years. One of the earliest seems to have been the tank built by B. F. Dillingham around 1898 at Woodlawn, his home at Beretania and Punahou Streets. A year later, a description of "the typical tropical home of the best class" in Honolulu observed that "a swimming pool completes the inducement to out-door life."

HJH (1982): 162–164.

Theaters and Plays

The earliest recorded performance of a play in the Islands took place during the stay of Archibald Campbell, who was a Honolulu resident from 1809 to 1810. Campbell wrote: "A theatre was erected under the direction of James Beattie, the king's block-maker, who had been at one time on the stage in England. . . . I was present on one occasion, at the performance of *Oscar and Malvina*. . . . The audience did not seem to understand the play well." A melodrama of Scottish life, the play starred the Hawaiian wife of Isaac Davis in the role of Malvina.

On January 17, 1834, some young Americans established the Oahu Amateur Theatre, an organization subsequently described as Honolulu's first community theater. Their first production, *Raising the Wind*, opened at the royal palace on March 5, 1834.

The first theater in Honolulu, according to *The Polynesian*, was the Thespian. This 275-seat structure opened September 11, 1847, at the corner of Maunakea and King Streets with a drama (*The Adopted Child*) and a farce (*Fortune's Frolic*).

The earliest theatrical performance by the College of Hawaii was a comedy, *The Revolving Wedge*, given in Punahou's Charles R. Bishop Hall on November 27, 1912.

The first public performance of the Footlights Club occurred April 28, 1915, in the Hawaiian Opera House. The play was Pinero's farce, *The Amazons*. The Footlights Club was reorganized as the Honolulu Community Theatre in December 1934. The following March, the new group offered its first production, *The Mikado*, at McKinley High School Auditorium.

HJH (1978): 101–102.

Toys

Children in pre-contact Hawai'i played a variety of games. They flew kites made of *hau* sticks covered with *kapa* cloth or pandanus leaves. They had swings made from morning-glory vines, spinning tops, and stilts. Noise makers included whistles and rattles. They also enjoyed a ring and ball game, a game resembling jacks, archery, and a dart game.

Hula ki'i, satiric Hawaiian puppet shows, were first described in 1820, although their origins may have dated from the late eighteenth century or earlier.

Western dolls, toys, and other playthings were introduced by early missionaries. A crude doll fashioned by Hiram Bingham for his daughter Lydia during the late 1830s has been described as Hawai'i's first doll, although other dolls included in the Mission Houses Museum collection may be as old or older. The collection also contains a good deal of doll house furniture, tiny dishes and chamber pots, and similar playthings intended for girls, mostly undated but apparently in large part from the 1825–1850 period. Items meant for boys include a humming top, toy cannons, a Chinese puzzle, miniature dominoes, and cardboard figures of Napoleon's cavalry officers.

Feher, Joesting, and Bushnell (1969): 115; Luomala (1984): 2, 3, 5; Evelyn MacDougal, "Hawaii's First Doll," undated pamphlet in HMCS Library, c. 1920; Mission Houses Museum, card index.

VCRs and Video Games

Although television sets were sold in Hawai'i as early as 1952, equipment for taping and reshowing programs, home showing of commercial movies, and playing video games was not available until the early 1970s.

The *Oahu Telephone Directory* Yellow Pages first listed videotapes in 1965 and video recorders in 1969. The earliest directory reference to VCRs (video cassette recorders made by Philips-Norelco) appeared in 1975. Two years later, a Honolulu video store, UCR, began to run newspaper ads for RCA/SelectaVision VCRs, apparently the first make to be heavily promoted in the Islands.

Stores selling or renting movies for home video use quickly multiplied.

Video games likewise appeared in the mid-1970s. The 1975 Yellow Pages listed both Consolidated Wholesale Distributors and Video Games of Hawaii as sources, and a year later Sears advertised the Pong TV Game for $59.99.

Oahu Telephone Directory, yellow pages for 1965 (p. 323), 1969 (p. 432), Dec. 1975 (p. 25–26, 39), and Dec. 1977 (p. 451); HA, 1 Dec. 1977, B3; HA, 1 Dec. 1978, B7; SSB&A, 5 Dec. 1976, A6.

YMCA and YWCA

The first meeting of the Young Men's Christian Association of Honolulu took place in Olympic Hall on April 30, 1869. Six months later, the group opened its reading rooms in the Sailor's

Home, and in 1883 the first Honolulu YMCA building was dedicated. In November of that year, the organization affiliated with the International YMCA.

The Hawaii Chapter of the Young Women's Christian Association was organized April 30, 1900. In 1912, it joined the national association. The Richards Street YWCA building, designed by Julia Morgan of San Francisco and opened in 1927, was the first significant building in Hawai'i to be built by a female architect.

Allen (1969): 2, 71, 213; H, Nov. 1988, 90–93; HA, 25 Aug. 1988, C1, C2.

Zoos

Kaimuki Zoo, apparently Hawai'i's earliest, opened at Wai'alae Road and Koko Head Avenue near the end of the streetcar line in 1905. An advertisement in the 1905–1906 city directory listed its attractions: "Animals, fish, birds, etc., Japanese tea house, Hawaiian grass houses, vaudeville Wednesday and Saturday nights, dancing every evening."

The Honolulu Zoo was established around 1914 in Kapi'olani Park with a modest collection of birds and animals. Two years later, an elephant was added, but the zoo remained something of a municipal stepchild until 1947, when it was given its first director.

The Honolulu Zoo elephant was not the city's first encounter with exotic fauna, however. A circus—Rowe's "Olympic"—entertained Islanders as early as December 1850. Even earlier, in 1841, a Kamchatka bear was brought to Honolulu for exhibit. Proving too fractious for local tastes, "Major Ursa" was eventually bludgeoned, shot, stripped of his coat, and converted into bear steaks. Five years later, a visiting ship presented some townsmen with a grizzly; this bear likewise encountered a lack of aloha, winding up as the chief participant in a barbecue.

HJH (1978): 101; HJH (1993): 243.

Art and Music

Art Exhibitions

The first organized art exhibition in Hawai'i was held in Honolulu in May 1882, as a benefit for the building fund of the Honolulu Library Association. The exhibition catalog listed 1,337 items.

Honolulu's first "Art Mart," exhibiting the work of Island artists along the Honolulu Zoo fence on Monsarrat Avenue, took place on Lei Day, May 1, 1954. It quickly became a regular weekend feature at that location.

Forbes (1992a): 176; Forbes (1992b): 74; *HSB*, 3 Apr. 1954; *HSB*, 25 Aug. 1954.

Artists

Native art, in the form of petroglyphs and carved images, flourished in pre-contact Hawai'i, but such art was anonymous.

Engraving of a Hawaiian war canoe by John Webber, the first artist of record to portray the Islands. AH.

The first professional artist to work in Hawai'i was John Webber, the official artist on Captain James Cook's third voyage. Webber's watercolors of Hawaiian scenes, made in 1778 and 1779, became the source of engravings illustrating the account of the voyage and have been frequently reproduced during the past two centuries.

For more than half a century, Island art was dominated by men like Webber, who were attached to expeditions that briefly visited Hawai'i and then moved on.

The first resident artists were members of the Protestant mission in the 1830s. Mostly untrained amateurs, they sometimes sketched Island scenes. One of the most skilled was Edward Bailey, a teacher at Lahainaluna, Maui, who sketched numerous scenes for his students to engrave. He lived on Maui from 1839 until 1885.

Eventually, Hawai'i attracted professional artists who established permanent residence in the Kingdom. Early examples include Paul Emmert, who arrived in 1853, Charles Furneaux, who arrived in 1880, and Jules Tavernier, who came in 1884.

The earliest native artist of consequence was Joseph Nawahi (1842–1896), one of the few Hawaiians attracted to painting prior to the twentieth century.

Haar and Neogy (1974): xi–xvi; Barrow (1978): 42–43, 49, 57, 95–98, 104; Feher, Joesting, and Bushnell (1969): 151, 153, 155, 179–180; Day (1984): 6, 44, 119; Forbes (1992a): 95, 161–162.

Bands

Hawaiians were introduced to Western instrumental music when Captain James Cook's men played the French horn, violin, and "german-flute" for them in January 1779. Visiting ships' bands presented concerts to the Hawaiians throughout the nineteenth century.

In 1843, Hilo residents assembled in the Reverend Coan's church to hear what has been described as the first concert given in Hawai'i by a complete orchestra. The concert was performed by the full brass band from the frigate United States.

Captain Henry Berger and his Royal Hawaiian Band, posing on the steps of Iolani Palace. AH.

The earliest resident musical group was the King's Oahu Band, which performed for some foreigners as early as January 1, 1816.

The forerunner of today's Royal Hawaiian Band, the King's Band, was formed in 1836 and maintained a somewhat fitful existence for the next third of a century. Reorganized in late 1870, it presented its first concert under its long-time leader, Captain Henry Berger, on June 11, 1872. (See also *Symphony Orchestras*.)

HJH (1978): 104; HJH (1990): 69–90; Lyman (1906): 99–100, 102–103.

Broadway Hit

The first hit song composed in Hawai'i for a Broadway musical comedy was Noel Coward's "A Room With a View," included in *This Year of Grace* in 1928. Coward framed both words and music while he sunned at Mokuleia Beach during a six-week stay in 1927.

Coward (1937): 261–161, 285–286; Morley (1969): 152, 167, 170–171.

Shipboard shot of Noel Coward during a 1930s Hawai'i visit. AH.

Dance and Ballet

Dance and ballet performances—aside from the traditional Hawaiian hula—were extremely rare in Hawai'i before 1900. After 1900, amateur groups occasionally offered dance recitals, as did some

Island schools. Professional ballet performances, however, remained largely nonexistent well into the twentieth century.

On January 17, 1916, the De Folco Grand Opera Company began a series of thirty-one performances at the Opera House. Unlike earlier touring troupes, the company included a six-member corps de ballet, which appeared in such staples as *Aida*, *La Gioconda*, and *Faust*. After the company's opening night, the *Bulletin* commented, "The corps de ballet are shapely, graceful dancers. Emilia Costanza, premiere danseuse, . . . created a mild sensation by appearing barefoot and sans tights."

Major ballet companies apparently did not include Honolulu in their travels until 1939, when the Covent Garden Ballet Russe, sailing from Australia to the West Coast, played two evenings at the McKinley High School Auditorium. The troupe danced *Spectre de la Rose*, *Swan Lake*, and other works (mostly in excerpt form) to music provided by the Honolulu Symphony Orchestra before elegantly dressed audiences.

Twenty-five years later, in 1964, dance enthusiasts organized Hawaiʻi's first resident ballet company, the Honolulu Ballet Theater. Joined by two artists from Hungary, the troupe made its debut the week before Christmas with a production of *The Nutcracker*.

HSB, 18 Jan. 1916, 9; HSB, 2 Mar. 1916, 7; HSB, 10 May 1939, 1, 4, 16; HA, 11 May 1939, 5; HSB, 11 May 1939, 3; HA, 23 Sept. 1964, C2; HA, 22 Oct. 1964, A1, A2; HSB, 16 Dec. 1964, E3; SSB&A, 20 Dec. 1964, A16.

Musical Societies

The Amateur Musical Society (also called Musical Amateur Society or just Musical Society) was formed in 1853 and met monthly for a number of years. On December 29, 1859, the group performed a vocal and instrumental concert at the Fort Street Church. The program included "The Heavens Are Telling" from Haydn's *The Creation*, apparently the first oratorio music heard in the Islands.

HJH (1978): 104–105.

Music and words first appeared together in print in Hawaiian Hymns and Music, 1837. *HMCS/MHM.*

Music Printing

Musical staffs and notation appeared for the first time in an instructional manual and hymnal published in 1834, *O Ke Kumu Leomele* (The rules of music).

Forbes (1992b): 76; Day and Loomis (1973): 12.

Operas

On Saturday evening, February 11, 1854, the Varieties Theatre on King Street presented Honolulu's earliest opera performance, Donizetti's *Daughter of the Regiment*. The cast of eight local performers was led by Mrs. D. W. Waller, wife of the theater's stage manager, who played the role of Madelaine. The theater bill makes no mention of the musical accompaniment, which was presumably provided by a lone pianist. *Daughter* shared the evening with a tragedy by Maturin, *The Sicilian Pirate*, and thus was probably offered in a severely cut version.

The first professional operatic performance in the Islands took place April 4, 1862, at the Royal Hawaiian Theater. Signor and Signora Bianchi, Miss Herrmann, Signor Grossi, and Mr. Gregg, en route from Sydney, Australia, to San Francisco, presented selections from Verdi's *Il Trovatore*.

Not until 1871 did Honolulu audiences see an opera presented in its entirety. Between October 7 and November 1 of that year, Madame Agatha States' Italian Opera (apparently a small group of professionals aided on occasion by local talent) performed *Ernani*, *Lucia di Lammermoor*, *Il Trovatore*, and other works. Some of the works were severely cut, but others appear to have been offered in full-length form. The musical accompaniment was still limited to a single pianist.

The earliest Hawaiian operas were two works performed in 1925. The first was *Pele and Lohi'au*, written by Fred Beckley and performed at the Hawaii Theater on April 16. The second was *Prince of Hawaii*, by Charles E. King, which was performed at the Liberty Theater on May 4.

HJH (1978): 105; HJH (1993): 241.

Photography

Island residents saw their first camera twenty-six years before the arrival of photography in Hawai'i. Jacques Etienne Victor Arago, draftsman on the De Freycinet expedition to the Islands in 1819, reported that he "showed Riouriou a Camera-obscura." The camera obscura, an ancestor of the modern reflex camera, was a filmless device for facilitating the sketching of scenes.

The earliest likenesses of Hawai'i residents were the daguerreotypes made of Timoteo Haalilio and William Richards when the two men were in Paris on a diplomatic mission in 1843. Copies are in the collection of the Bernice Pauahi Bishop Museum.

Daguerreotype of Timoteo Haalilio made during a diplomatic mission to Paris in 1843. This is the earliest known photograph of a Hawaiian. AH.

The first Island photographer, Theophilus Metcalf, ran an advertisement in *The Polynesian* for a five-month period in 1845, offering "to take likenesses by the Daguerreotype method . . . for $10 a picture." No known examples of Metcalf's photographs still exist.

The first camera advertised for sale in the Islands was described as "a daguerreotype apparatus, with Chemicals complete." The ad was placed by S. H. Williams & Company in *The Polynesian* in 1848.

The Honolulu Almanac and Directory, 1886, first used half-tone engravings to reproduce photographs of Island scenes, including a portrait of King Kalakaua and views of Iolani Palace and other local sights. The earliest half-tones used in Honolulu newspapers appeared in the *Evening Bulletin* on September 30, November 11, and December 2, 1899.

Amateur photography began to flourish in the late 1800s. The first retail establishments with camera counters were two Fort Street drug stores, Hollister & Company and Benson, Smith & Company, both in 1887. The first business establishment to advertise "printing done for amateurs" was the studio of Theo. P. Severin in 1888. The first camera club, the Hawaiian Camera Club, was organized January 10, 1889, with Christian J. Hedemann as its first president.

Island photographers were experimenting with color photography and processing as early as the 1920s. On January 24, 1924, for example, F. E. Stafford of *The Advertiser* showed color prints of flowers, a rainbow, and Kaua'i scenery before a meeting of the Hawaiian Trail and Mountain Club.

HJH (1978): 102–103, 112–113; HJH (1987): 156–157; HJH (1993): 241; HHR, Oct. 1967, 409–416; Arago (1823): 136; P, 1 July 1848, 27; Davis (1980): 16, 39–40; Davis (1988): 90; HA, 25 Jan. 1924, 1.

Pianos

Pianos first reached Hawai'i during the 1830s. F. J. F. Meyen, an 1831 visitor to O'ahu, wrote that "one finds varnished floors, the finest furniture, and beautiful pianos in the missionaries' homes." An 1832 list of mission furnishings, however, failed to mention a piano.

Sereno Bishop, writing in 1899, recalled seeing one in the house of a Mrs. Perkins, near Union Street, not later than 1836.

The first advertisement offering a piano for sale ("1 superior Piano-Forte") was placed by Henry Paty & Company in the *Sandwich Island Gazette* on September 10, 1836.

Meyen (1981): 70; information from Lela Goodell, HMCS Library, 27 Sept. 1982; F, Feb. 1899, 16.

Symphony Orchestras

Although the Royal Hawaiian Band and other early groups often played operatic overtures, concert waltzes, and similar light classical compositions, serious symphonic music was virtually unknown in the Islands before the 1880s. The Symphony Club, founded in 1881 and composed at one time of fourteen pieces, was the only attempt at orchestral symphony music. However, the group broke up three years later.

The first full-scale symphony orchestra in the Islands was the Amateur Orchestra (also called the YMCA Orchestra), organized in 1895. As many as twenty-four musicians performed in its concerts, usually under the direction of Wray Taylor. The Amateur Orchestra was active until 1902, when many of its members moved to the newly organized Honolulu Symphony Orchestra.

The Honolulu Symphony Orchestra made its first appearance at a smoking concert given at the club house in October 1902 in honor of the officers of the German cruiser *Cormoran*. The principal number on the program was Mozart's Symphony in G Minor. This concert appears to have been a private affair before members of the Honolulu Symphony Society and specially invited guests.

The orchestra's first public performance took place at the Hawaiian Opera House on May 2, 1903, with W. F. Jocher leading twenty-nine musicians in Schubert's Unfinished Symphony and shorter works by Bach, Mozart, Mascagni, and Wagner. (See also *Bands*.)

HJH (1978): 105–106; HJH (1986): 172–187.

Ukuleles

The modern ukulele was adapted from a Portuguese instrument called the braguinha, introduced to Hawai'i by the first group of Portuguese immigrants in 1878. No one in this group was able to play the instrument, however. Thus, ukulele history did not really begin until the second boatload of immigrants arrived on August 22, 1879. On board were musicians who could play the instrument, as well as craftsmen who could make it.

The earliest local manufacturer of the ukulele was apparently Augusto Dias. In 1884, Dias opened a shop on King Street for making and repairing the ukulele, guitar, and other musical instruments.

Kanahele (1979): 394–395, 397–398.

Sports

Baseball

Various forerunners of the modern game of baseball appear to have been played in Hawai'i well before 1860. In 1840, *The Polynesian* referred to "good old bat-and-ball." Frank Boardman wrote in 1910 that in Honolulu "a form of baseball had been played as far back as 1842 under the name of rounders, one-old-cat, two-old-cat and townball." Curtis J. Lyons was quoted in 1901 as saying that the boys at Punahou were the first to play baseball in the Islands after it had been introduced by a Boston clergyman in the early 1840s.

The earliest newspaper reference to baseball appears to have occurred in *The Polynesian* on April 7, 1860: "Quite an interesting game of ball came off yesterday afternoon on the Esplanade between the Punahou Boys and the Town Boys. . . . The 'boys' of a larger growth, among whom were some of the leading merchants and their clerks, had a game of good old-fashioned base ball on Sheriff Brown's premises. . . ." This game preceded another on the Esplanade, also credited with being the first recorded game, by more than seven years.

Major league teams first came to Hawai'i for exhibitions in November 1888, when the Chicago and All-America teams briefly stopped in Honolulu in the course of a world tour. The scheduled double-header at Makiki recreation grounds had to be canceled, however, when their ship arrived a day late and the Sunday blue laws took effect.

Honolulu finally obtained a minor league professional baseball franchise, the Pacific Coast League, on January 12, 1961. Three months later, a crowd of 6,041 watched the new Hawaii Islanders and the Vancouver Mounties open the PCL season at Honolulu Stadium. This game, the first professional league game in Island history, was won by Hawaii, 4-3.

P, 26 Dec. 1840, 114; HJH (1978): 109–110; PCA, 24 Nov. 1888, 3; PCA, 26 Nov. 1888, 3; HA, 28 Nov. 1988, A3.

Baseball Players

The first baseball player to live in Hawai'i was Alexander Joy Cartwright. Whether or not he ever played a game in the Islands, however, is uncertain.

While a resident of New York, Cartwright laid out the modern baseball diamond (a square thirty paces on each side), wrote the game's first playing rules, and in 1846 organized the Knickerbocker Baseball Club.

Cartwright left New York a few years later, traveling first to the California gold mines and then to Honolulu in 1849. He became a commission merchant and in 1851 founded the Honolulu Fire Department.

On April 6, 1865, he wrote to a former Knickerbockers teammate: "Charlie, I have in my possession the original ball with which we used to play on Murray Hill. Many is the pleasant hours [sic] I have had after it, on Mountain and Prairie, and many an equally pleasant ours [sic] on the sunny plains of 'Hawaii nei,' here in Honolulu, my pleasant Island home." This suggests that he may have

Alexander Joy Cartwright, a key figure in the development of baseball, was also a founder and chief of the Honolulu Fire Department. AH.

continued playing after moving to Hawai'i. In any event, he is known to have been a spectator at Punahou's baseball games.

The first Hawai'i-born baseball player to play in the major leagues, John Brodie ("Honolulu Johnny") Williams pitched four games for the Detroit Tigers in 1914. Born in Honolulu in 1889, he later returned to the Islands and worked for the City and County Refuse Department.

Reichler (1982): 9, 2085; *PP*, May 1947, 24; *HA*, 5 Oct. 1990, C2; *New York Times*, 4 Oct. 1990, A1, A20; Nellist (1925): 82; *H*, Sept. 1977, 57–61, 91–92; letter from Cartwright to Charles S. Debort (or DeBort), New York, in Cartwright Collection, AH; *F*, Mar. 1924, 70; *HSB*, 21 Oct. 1960, 19.

Baseball Reporting

The earliest newspaper accounts of Island baseball games were published by *The Polynesian* on April 7, 1860, and by *The Advertiser* on June 6, 1867. These articles described informal and apparently unscheduled contests played by pick-up teams on the Honolulu Esplanade.

In May 1889, the two Honolulu dailies initiated weekly descriptions of the games of the five-team Hawaii Baseball League, accompanied by detailed box scores and the current team won-lost records and standings.

Also at this time, the *Bulletin* began paying attention—limited, sporadic, and with long time lags imposed by the slow communications of the time—to mainland baseball news. On May 16, 1889, the paper carried the National League and American Association standings, correct to May 5.

The opening of cable service to California in January 1903 permitted the speedy transmission of sporting news, but its use for baseball scores was at first quite limited.

The situation improved considerably after the establishment of commercial radio telegraph service in July 1912. Both dailies carried page-one accounts of the 1912 World Series games. A year later, *The Advertiser* published box scores of the World Series contests, apparently the first to appear for mainland baseball games. Play-by-play reports were in evidence by 1916.

Not until 1955, however, did box scores for regular season games become a daily feature, first for the *Star-Bulletin* and a year later for *The Advertiser*.

DB, 13 May 1889, 3; PCA, 20 May 1889, 3; DB, 27 May 1889, 3; DB, 16 May 1889, 2; PCA, 14 Oct. 1903, 1; EB, 14 Oct. 1903, 2; PCA, 15 Oct. 1912, 1; HSB, 15 Oct. 1912, 1, 9; PCA, 17 Oct. 1912, 1; PCA, 8 Oct. 1913, 1; PCA, 10 Oct. 1916, 6; HSB, 22 Apr. 1955, 19; HA, 18 Apr. 1956, C2.

Basketball

Basketball apparently came to Hawai'i soon after annexation. "Basketball is booming," reported *The Advertiser* on February 21, 1899. "Three teams have already been organized and a fourth is in contemplation." The three organized teams were the Business Men, the Unknowns, and the Rough Riders.

Basketball quickly became popular at Island schools. On March 28, 1902, for example, the Oahu College (now Punahou School) girls beat the YWCA, 19-17. The first basketball game played by the College of Hawaii was held at the YMCA on the evening of February 1, 1913, when the College beat McKinley High School, 14-13.

The Hawaii Pacific College Sea Warriors won Hawai'i's first national basketball championship when they defeated Oklahoma Baptist, 88-83, in the National Association of Intercollegiate Athletics championship on March 22, 1993.

HJH (1978): 110; HJH (1993): 239; HA, 24 Mar. 1993, A1, C1, C4.

Bikinis

The first-known bikini wearer in Hawai'i was photographed by Morris Fox on Waikīkī Beach in front of the Surfrider Hotel in January 1952.

HJH, (1987): 156.

Waikīkī's first known bikini swimming suit, photographed by Morris Fox on the beach by the Surfrider Hotel in January 1952.

Boardsailing

Boardsailing, also called freesailing, sailboarding, and windsurfing, apparently had its origins in Hawai'i in the 1930s. In 1935, Tom Blake experimented with various sailing rigs attached to his hollow surfboard and published photographs of such craft sailing off Waikīkī Beach. In March 1941, the first official surfboard sailing race was held off Waikīkī's Outrigger Canoe Club.

Much later, in 1967, the new windsurfer—radically redesigned—became popular first in Europe and then in the United States. Within a few years, Kailua Beach was acclaimed as one of the best freesailing areas in the world, and in 1978, it was the site of Hawai'i's first World Cup Windsurfing Championship.

PP, Feb. 1935, 21–22; Blake (1935): 95, photos after 64; Lueras (1984): 200; Gadd, Boothroyd, and Durrell (1980); Hall (1985): 10; *HA*, 24 Feb. 1978, F4; *HSB*, 28 Feb. 1978, F5; *HSB*, 27 Mar. 1979, C4; *HA*, 16 Aug. 1985, C1, C4.

Boxing

Hawai'i's first world boxing champion, Salvador "Dado" Marino, won the flyweight title at age thirty-four or thirty-five in a fight with Terry Allen before 10,762 fans at Honolulu Stadium on August 1, 1950. He lost his title to Yoshio Shirai in Tokyo in May 1952 and retired six months later with a 57-14-3 record. Marino was born in Olowalu, Maui.

HA, 1 Nov. 1989, C1; *HSB*, 2 Nov. 1989, D1, D2.

Football

Football appears to have been introduced to Hawai'i around 1875, when Amasa Pratt bought a football for the boys at Punahou and taught them "a form of Association football." By 1887, they were playing St. Alban's College (the forerunner of Iolani School).

Newspaper accounts of local games appeared as early as 1884, when Fort Street School beat Punchbowl School at the Makiki Reserve, "by two goals to nothing." As late as 1893, however, *The Advertiser* felt obliged to provide its readers with a detailed description of the rules in advance of a forthcoming game.

On October 23, 1909, the College (now University) of Hawaii played its first football game. The College defeated McKinley High School, 6-5, and finished the 1909 season with a 2-2 record, entirely against McKinley and Punahou.

Bowl games in Hawai'i originated with the New Year's Day games traditionally scheduled by the University of Hawai'i as the concluding matches on its annual schedules. The first of these was the Oregon State game played at Mō'ili'ili Field on January 1, 1924. The University of Hawai'i won, 7-0.

These annual affairs remained unnamed until January 1, 1936, when a newspaper headline announced, "Rainbows-Trojans in Poi Bowl Classic Today." In 1939, the Poi Bowl became the Pineapple Bowl.

The first Islander to play in the National Football League, Walter Tin Kit "Sneeze" Achiu, became a sports star at St. Louis College in Honolulu and later at the University of Dayton. In 1926, he joined the Dayton Triangles of the NFL for $125 per game.

HJH (1978): 110; PCA, 1 Dec. 1884, 3; HA, 2 Jan. 1924, 9; HA, 1 Jan. 1936, 10; HA, 2 Jan. 1936, 8; HA, 1 Jan. 1939, 10; HA, 3 Jan. 1939, 1; information from David Kittelson, University of Hawai'i Library, 6 Jan. 1986; HA, 24 Mar. 1989, C7.

Golf

In what may have been the earliest newspaper reference to golf in Hawai'i, *The Advertiser* reported on January 3, 1896: "The grow-ing interest in golf in this city has resulted in the formation of a club which is composed of President Dole, Mrs. Graham, Mrs. Renjes, Mrs. McGraw, Captain Broome and Walter Dillingham. . . . The hilly ground immediately back of Punahou has been thought a good place for the links and will probably be adapted to the game of golf." There is no evidence that anything ever came of either this club or its proposed golf course.

The first golf course actually constructed opened in Moanalua in 1898. In a 1901 newspaper story, S. E. Damon, on whose father's land the links were located, said, "The course has been shortened from 18 to 9 holes because it has been conceded by the majority of players that the latter number is sufficient for a warm climate such as we have here. . . . I might say that, since the new arrangement was instituted a short time ago, there have been more players out than ever before."

The Hawaiian Open was first held November 3–9, 1965, at Waialae Country Club golf course. The purse that year was $50,000, including $9,000 for the winner. By 1993, the total had increased to $1,200,000, and the winner received $216,000.

HJH (1978): 110–111; Hitch and Kuramoto (1981): 160–161; SHDB 1986: 246; SHDB 1992: 225.

Hang Gliding

Hang gliding was introduced to Hawai'i in April 1973, and by summer approximately thirty Islanders had taken up the sport. The first fatality occurred March 18, 1974, when a downdraft caused James Michael Phillips, a twenty-three-year-old Kahaluu resident, to crash behind the Hawaii Kai Golf Course. (See also *Gliders* under *TRANSPORTATION*.)

HA, 19 Mar. 1974, A1.

Marathons

Out of 167 entrants, 151 finished the first Honolulu Marathon on December 16, 1973. Duncan McDonald of Kailua had the winning time of 2:27:34.8.

The Diamond Head Run, sometimes described as a marathon, actually extended only five miles. It was first run in 1924. (See also *Triathlons*.)

HSB, 17 Dec. 1973, A1, C3; HSB, 21 Nov. 1931, 11.

Polo

The first polo match played in Hawai'i took place in Honolulu on November 3, 1880. The game was played at Pālama, between the officers of HMS *Gannet* and some local residents.

PP, June 1940, 9; HG, 10 Nov. 1880, 3; Forecast (Outrigger Canoe Club), May 1951, 4, 11.

Roller Skating

Williams and Wallace opened the first roller skating rink in the Islands in Buffum's Hall on Hotel Street on July 22, 1871. The grand opening, attended by Queen Emma, included a program featuring a march, lancers, two quadrilles, and a Virginia reel, all danced on skates. Thereafter, the Honolulu Skating Rink operated five nights a week, charging skaters twenty-five cents an hour and spectators twenty-five cents an evening.

HJH (1978): 113.

Skateboarding

Skateboards first became popular in Hawai'i around 1963, but the fad soon fizzled. Then, in 1973, a young surfer named Frank Nasworthy began experimenting with the polyurethane wheels used in expensive roller skates. By early 1975, skateboarding had again become an Island craze.

HJH (1978): 113.

Skiing

Winter sports in Hawai'i date at least to 1840, when James Jackson Jarves, editor of *The Polynesian*, wrote that "in the course of his jaunt [to the island of Hawai'i] he has snow-balled on Mauna Kea. . . ."

Skiing came much later. Perhaps the first evidence of this sport was an uncaptioned photograph of a skier published in *Paradise of the Pacific* in December 1933.

"However, it was not until the winter of 1935–36 that skiing actually took place in Hawaii," according to L. W. Bryan. "A heavy fall of snow in February of 1936 and the fact that Dudley Lewis' skis were available, made it possible for the writer and his son to become pioneers in this sport in Hawaii. . . . At 9:00 a.m., on February 7th we were skiing on Mauna Kea . . . [at] an elevation of 9,500 feet near Halepohaku. . . ." By February 1938, two ski clubs had been formed, one on the island of Hawai'i and the other on O'ahu.

HJH (1978): 111.

Skin Diving and Scuba Equipment

An 1840 Honolulu newspaper item first recorded the local use of modern diving equipment: "Thousands have daily lined the wharves to witness the carpenter, Mr. Dibble, in his novel suit of india-rubber with a glass helmet disappear beneath the surface of the water. Air is communicated to him by a forcing pump, and by means of copper rods his wants are made known to those above." Dibble was inspecting a ship's bottom.

Underwater vision, a matter of considerable interest to Island divers and spearfishers, received little help until recent times. The ancient Hawaiians, who often dove to great depths, did all their underwater viewing with the naked eye, unprotected by goggles or face masks. By 1901, glass-bottomed viewing boxes were common in the Islands, but most divers continued to swim without eye protection well into the twentieth century.

The earliest published references to diving goggles appeared in the 1920s. William G. Anderson, a member of the *Tanager* expedition, was photographed wearing goggles at Laysan Island in 1923, and Ted Dranga was similarly pictured, seeking coral on an O'ahu beach, a few years later.

Modern face masks were in use in the Islands by the end of the 1930s. In July 1938, *Paradise of the Pacific* published a photograph of two girls in swimming suits, one wearing goggles and the other equipped with a face mask and spears.

In 1943, the Navy set up an Underwater Demolition Team (UDT) school on O'ahu and later moved it to Kama'ole, Maui. Before the first group of volunteers had completed their training at the O'ahu school, about twenty of the best were rushed to the invasion fleet on its way to capture Kwajalein. The frogmen, initially supplied only with goggles and knives, eventually were given face masks and swim fins, but breathing apparatus remained unavailable until after the war.

Civilian divers in Hawai‘i began using modern skin-diving equipment in the late 1940s and early 1950s. One of the first, Wally Young, began taking underwater photographs in 1948. Flippers and face masks became common around 1950, followed somewhat later by snorkels. By 1951, oceanographers from the University of Hawai‘i regularly used Aqua-Lungs.

HJH (1978): 112; HJH (1985): 139–141.

Sports Stadiums

Honolulu Stadium, the first large sports stadium in the Islands, opened on November 11, 1926, at King and Isenberg Streets. In the stadium's first game, 12,000 football fans watched Town Team defeat the University of Hawai‘i, 14-7.

A new 50,000-seat, $32 million facility opened in Hālawa, O‘ahu, on September 13, 1975. Aloha Stadium boasted stands that could be moved to different configurations (depending on the sport) on a film of air. Although a few other stadiums in the United States offered movable bleachers, none at that time used this unique air-bearing system. (See also *Baseball* and *Football*.)

Bill Gee, "Only the Memories Remain," SSB&A, 11 July 1976, C1; HJH (1981): 108.

Sumo Wrestling

Sumo wrestling was introduced to Hawai‘i on February 11, 1885, when a group of Japanese immigrants at the Immigration Depot engaged in a series of matches witnessed by the king and other notables. Two teams, each consisting of twenty amateur wrestlers, competed for the prize—ten tubs of "sahkee," a popular Japanese drink.

In 1972, at the Nagoya sumo tournament, a native Hawaiian,

Jesse James Walani Kuhaulua (known professionally as Takamiyama), became the first non-Japanese national sumo champion.

In early 1993, another native Hawaiian, Chadwick Haheo Rowan, under the name Akebono, rose even higher to become the first non-Japanese *yokozuna*, or sumo grand champion (the sport's highest rank), in history.

PCA, 12 Feb. 1885, 3; Sandoz (1992): 11–12, 31–32; HA, 27 May 1993, C1, C7; HSB, 9 June 1993, D1.

Surfing

A highly developed and popular sport among the ancient Hawaiians, surfboard riding was first observed by Westerners when Captain James Cook and his crew arrived. John Webber's panoramic view of the *Resolution* and the *Discovery* at anchor in Kealakekua Bay, January 17, 1779, includes the first Western image of a surf-boarder.

After a decline in popularity that lasted more than a century, renewed interest in surfboard riding began to develop in the early 1900s. One of the leading riders in this period was Duke Kahanamoku, the champion swimmer. Another noted surfer was George Freeth, an Irish-Hawaiian, who went to California in 1907 to demonstrate surfing. Staying on, he did much to encourage the sport on the West Coast.

Surfboard design continued to evolve over the years. Major contributions included the hollow board and fin, both credited to Tom Blake (1929). After Blake patented this hollow board, it was produced by the Robert Mitchell Manufacturing Company of Cincinnati. (See also *Boardsailing.*)

Lueras (1984): 30–49, 217; Blake (1935): 51, 67–68, 90; Young (1983): 43–45, 49; PP, Dec. 1931, 45–52.

Swimming the Moloka'i Channel

William K. Pai, the first person to swim the Kaiwi Channel, reportedly swam from 'Īlio Point on Moloka'i to the Blowhole near O'ahu's Sandy Beach on August 25 and 26, 1939—a claim once treated by some newsmen with skepticism.

The first woman to swim the channel was Robin Isayama, on September 29, 1994.

HA, 27 Aug. 1939, 6; HA, 26 Apr. 1961, B1; HA, 27 Apr. 1961, A14; HA, 28 Apr. 1961, A12; HSB, 27 Apr. 1961, 1, 1A; HA, 30 Sept. 1994, A1, A6; HSB, 30 Sept. 1994, D1, D2.

Tennis

Tennis in Hawai'i has been traced to the 1880s and early 1890s, when it was mostly limited to the English in Honolulu who held tennis teas. An 1894 match between an American and a Hawaiian

Lawn tennis at the McKibbin residence, Miller and Beretania Streets, around 1880. HHS.

and two Englishmen (the English unexpectedly lost) stimulated interest in the sport, and soon after, the Pacific Tennis Club was formed.

The first Island championship was held under the newly created Hawaiian Lawn Tennis Association in 1895.

HJH (1978): 113; Scott (1968): 211; Husted Honolulu directories, 1896–1897 to 1916.

Transpac Yacht Race

The Transpac race, from California to Honolulu, is the best known of several yacht races involving Hawai'i. A biennial event, it was first run in June 1906 with only three vessels entered. *Lurline* was the winner.

Smock (1980): 24–34.

Triathlons

The Bud Light Ironman Triathlon World Championship was first run in Hawai'i in 1978, with fifteen registrants and twelve finishers. By 1986, there were 1,039 registrants, of whom 951 finished the race. (See also *Marathons*.)

SHDB 1987: 259.

Special Foods
and Drinks

Alcoholic Beverages

Alcoholic beverages were unknown to pre-contact Hawaiians. The earliest appearance was recorded by David Samwell at Kaua'i on January 21, 1778.

The next mention of alcohol occurred thirteen years later. According to Kamakau, "The first taste that Kamehameha and his people had of rum was at Kailua in 1791 or perhaps a little earlier, brought in by Captain Maxwell. Kamehameha went out to the ship with Young and Davis when it was sighted off Keahole Point and there they all drank rum. . . . Then nothing would do but Ka-lani-moku must get some of this sparkling water, and he was the first chief to buy rum."

In 1802, John Turnbull learned from John Young that "some

convicts from Botany Bay, having effected their escape to the Sand-wich Islands, rendered themselves at first serviceable to Tamahama [Kamehameha], and, in recompence, were put in possession of small portions of land for cultivation. On these they raised some sugar-canes, and from them at last contrived to distill a sort of spirit, with which they entertained each other by turns, keeping birth-days and other holidays. . . ." William Stevenson, or Stephenson, an escaped convict from New South Wales, has been identified by some as the first to introduce to the Islands a method of "distilling a spirit from the tee-root."

Within a decade or so, Island residents were producing liquor on a commercial basis. Several small distilleries were in operation by the 1820s. (See also *Bars* under COMMERCE and *Beer, Sake,* and *Wine*.)

HJH (1980): 87–88.

Beer

Don Francisco de Paula Marin, the first Island resident to brew beer, recorded in his journal on February 2, 1812, the making of "a barrel of beer."

Hawai'i's first full-scale brewery appeared in 1854. From April 15 to October 21, *The Polynesian* carried a weekly one-column advertisement headed "Honolulu Brewery—Genuine Beer." The copy continued, "The undersigned, having established a Brewry [sic] in Honolulu, Fort street, opposite the French Hotel, are now prepared to supply families, hotels, boarding houses and bar rooms, in bottles or in kegs. This Beer is made of barley and hops only—contains no alcohol, nor any ingredient whatever injurious to health. . . ." It was signed by J. J. Bischoff & Company. On October 28, 1854, the ad was retitled "Honolulu Brewery Malt Beer," and the reference to its non-alcoholic contents was deleted; in this form it ran until December 20, 1856.

Other breweries followed this initial effort. The Honolulu Brewing and Malting Company, Ltd., makers of Primo Beer, began production on February 13, 1901, and continued until the arrival of prohibition. Renamed Hawaii Brewing Company, the company resumed the manufacture of Primo in 1934 and operated until 1979 when it discontinued operation.

In October 1958, Primo was the first American beer to be marketed in aluminum cans. Although heavily promoted, the eleven-ounce "Shiny Steiny" failed to achieve popularity and was eventually withdrawn.

HJH (1980): 88–89.

Huli-Huli Chicken

Huli-Huli barbecued chicken, a favorite Island delicacy, first became popular in the late 1950s.

Ernie Morgado co-founded Pacific Poultry in 1955. For a meeting with farmers shortly thereafter, Morgado and his partner Mike Asagi marinated and barbecued chickens using a special sauce from Morgado's mother. Noting its success, Morgado began marketing this product, dubbed Huli-Huli Chicken, through presales by schools and charities. He registered the name as a trademark with the Territory in 1958 and the U.S. government in 1965.

Hawaii Magazine, July-Aug. 1993, 60–62.

Ice Cream

Ice cream, commercially available in New York City as early as 1786, was not sold in Honolulu until May 1870, when it was offered by the American Coffee Saloon. An ice-making machine, costing $100, was exhibited a year earlier, in July 1869.

Although historians attribute the first ice cream cone to the 1904 St. Louis Exposition, a competing claim has been made for Kaua'i. According to Dora Jane Isenberg Cole and Juliet Rice Wichman, Josephine Wundenberg King sometimes served ice cream to the ladies and children of the Hawaiian Sunday School at her home in Līhuʻe. Eventually, she began to notice that her spoons were disappearing after such affairs, so she asked a local Japanese baker to make senbei cookies rolled into cornucopias. No date has been offered for this innovation in crime prevention.

Kane (1981): 316; PCA, 28 May 1870, 2; PCA, 17 July 1869, 3; Cole and Wichman (1977): 25.

Marshmallows

The introduction of marshmallows to Hawaiʻi has been credited to Emma Louise Dillingham, who brought a large tin of marshmallows from San Francisco in October 1878.

Frear (1934): 265.

Sake

Sake, imported from Japan for many years, was manufactured locally beginning on November 17, 1908, when Tajiro Sumida founded the Honolulu Japanese Sake Brewing Company (later known as Honolulu Sake & Ice Company, Ltd., and the Honolulu Sake Brewery Company). At one time, a half-dozen sake breweries operated in the Islands. Sumida's firm suspended sake production during the prohibition era and again during World War II but eventually outlasted all its competitors, closing for good on December 31, 1992.

HA, 16 Nov. 1978, A3; *The Sales Builder*, Aug. 1940, 14; HSB, 11 Dec. 1992, B1.

Wine

Hawaiʻi's first wine producer was Don Francisco de Paula Marin. On February 24, 1815, he wrote in his journal, "This day we began to plant the King's vines." On July 6, 1815, he wrote, "This day I began to make wine and I drew off 38 gallons."

Gast and Conrad (1973): 49–51, 215–216.

References

Abramson, Joan. 1976. *Photographers of Old Hawaii*. Honolulu: Island Heritage, Ltd.

Adams, Romanzo. 1937. *Interracial Marriage in Hawaii*. New York: The Macmillan Co.

Alexander, Mary Charlotte, and Charlotte Peabody Dodge. 1941. *Punahou: 1841–1941*. Berkeley, CA, and Los Angeles: University of California Press.

Alexander, W. D. 1899. *A Brief History of the Hawaiian People*. New York, Cincinnati, and Chicago: American Book Co.

Allen, Gwenfread E. 1969. *The Y.M.C.A. in Hawaii, 1869–1969*. Honolulu: The Young Men's Christian Association.

Anderson, Judith Icke. 1981. *William Howard Taft, An Intimate History*. New York and London: W. W. Norton & Co.

Anon. 1834. *Alemanaka Hawaii. No Ka Makahiki o ko Kakou Haku o Iesu Kristo 1835*. Oʻahu: Na Na Misionari i Pai.

Arago, Jacques. 1823. *Narrative of a Voyage Round the World*. London: Treuttel and Wurtz, Treuttel, Jun., and Richter. Facsimile reprint 1971. Part II. Amsterdam, N. Israel, and New York: Da Capo Press.

Barnard, Charles H. 1829. *A Narrative of the Sufferings and Adventures of Capt. Charles H. Barnard in a Voyage Round the World during the Years 1812, 1814, 1815 & 1816*. New York: Privately printed.

Barrot, Theodore-Adolphe. 1978. *Unless Haste Is Made*. Translated by Daniel Dole. Kailua: Press Pacifica.

Barrow, Terence. 1978. *Captain Cook in Hawaii*. Honolulu: Island Heritage, Ltd.

Beaglehole, J. C., ed. 1967. *The Journals of Captain Cook on His Voyages of Discovery*, Vol. III, *The Voyages of the Resolution and Discovery, 1776–1780*, Parts One and Two. Cambridge: Published for the Hakluyt Society at the University Press.

Bennett, C. C. 1869. *Honolulu Directory, and Historical Sketch of the Hawaiian or Sandwich Islands*. Honolulu: Privately printed.

Berger, Andrew J. 1981. *Hawaiian Birdlife*. Second edition. Honolulu: University of Hawaiʻi Press.

Bingham, Hiram. 1849. *A Residence of Twenty-One Years in the Sandwich Islands*. Third edition. Hartford, CT.: Hezekiah Huntington; New York: Sherman Converse. Reprint 1981. Rutland, VT, and Tokyo: Charles E. Tuttle Co.

Blake, Tom. 1935. *Hawaiian Surfboard*. Honolulu: Paradise of the Pacific Press.

Blanding, Don. 1930. *Hula Moons*. New York: Dodd, Mead & Co.

Bryan, William Alanson. 1915. *Natural History to Hawaii*. Honolulu: The Hawaiian Gazette Co., Ltd.

Campbell, Archibald. 1967. *A Voyage Round the World from 1806 to 1812*. Facsimile reproduction of the third American edition of 1822. Honolulu: University of Hawai'i Press, for Friends of the Library of Hawaii.

Carr, Norma. 1980. *Puerto Rican: One Identity From a Multi-Ethnic Heritage*. Honolulu: Hawaii State Department of Education, Office of Instructional Services, General Education Branch.

Catton, Margaret M. L. 1959. *Social Service in Hawaii*. Palo Alto, CA: Pacific Books.

Cleveland, Richard J. 1842. *Narrative of Voyages and Commercial Enterprises*. Two volumes. Cambridge: John Owen.

Cole, Dora Jane Isenberg, and Juliet Rice Wichman. 1987. *Early Kauai Hospitality, A Family Cookbook of Receipts* [sic], *1820–1920*. Lihue: Kauai Museum Association, Ltd.

Condé, Jesse C., and Gerald M. Best. 1973. *Sugar Trains*. Felton, CA: Glenwood Publishers.

Cook, John. 1927. *Reminiscences of John Cook, Kamaaina and Forty-Niner*. Honolulu: New Freedom Press.

Coward, Noel. 1937. *Present Indicative*. Garden City, NY: Doubleday, Doran, and Co.

Davis, Lynn. 1980. *Na Pa'i Ki'i: The Photographers in the Hawaiian Islands, 1845–1900*. Honolulu: Bernice Pauahi Bishop Museum Press.

——, with Nelson Foster. 1988. *A Photographer in the Kingdom: Christian J. Hedemann's Early Images of Hawai'i*. Honolulu: Bernice Pauahi Bishop Museum Press.

Daws, Gavan. 1966. *Honolulu—The First Century: Influences in the Development of the Town to 1876*. Ph.D. dissertation, University of Hawai'i, 1966; Ann Arbor, MI: University Microfilms, 1971.

——. 1968. *Shoal of Time: A History of the Hawaiian Islands*. Reprint 1974. Honolulu: University of Hawai'i Press.

Day, A. Grove. 1984. *History Makers of Hawaii*. Honolulu: Mutual Publishing of Honolulu.

——, and Albertine Loomis. 1973. *Ka Pa'i Palapala, Early Printing in Hawaii*. Honolulu: Printing Industries of Hawaii.

Dean, Love. 1991. *The Lighthouses of Hawaii*. Honolulu: University of Hawai'i Press.

De Freycinet, Louis. 1978. *Hawaii in 1819: A Narrative Account by Louis Claude De Saulses de Freycinet*. Translated by Ella L. Wiswell and edited by Marion Kelly. Honolulu: Bernice Pauahi Bishop Museum, Department of Anthropology.

Degener, Otto. 1945. *Plants of Hawaii National Park*. Ann Arbor, MI: Edwards Brothers, Inc.

——. 1946. *Flora Hawaiiensis*. Four books. Second edition. Honolulu: Privately printed.

De Varigny, Charles. 1981. *Fourteen Years in the Sandwich Islands, 1855–1868*. Translated by Alfons L. Korn. Honolulu: University of Hawai'i Press.

Dibble, Sheldon. 1909. *A History of the Sandwich Islands.* Honolulu: Thomas G. Thrum.

Dorita, Sister Mary. 1975. *Filipino Immigration to Hawaii.* San Francisco: R & E Research Associates.

Eckert, J. E. 1951. *Rehabilitation of the Beekeeping Industry in Hawaii.* Honolulu: Industrial Research Advisory Council.

Elliott, Rex R., and Stephen C. Gould. 1988. *Hawaiian Bottles of Long Ago.* Revised edition, Honolulu: Hawaiian Service, Inc.

Ellis, William. 1969. *Polynesian Researches, Hawaii.* Rutland, VT, and Tokyo: Charles E. Tuttle Co.

Ewen, David. 1971. *The New Encyclopedia of the Opera.* New York: Hill and Wang.

——. 1982. *American Composers, A Biographical Dictionary.* New York: G. P. Putnam's Sons.

Feher, Joseph, Edward Joesting, and O. A. Bushnell. 1969. *Hawaii: A Pictorial History.* Honolulu: Bernice Pauahi Bishop Museum Press.

Fitzpatrick, Gary L. 1986. *The Early Mapping of Hawai'i.* Honolulu: Editions Limited.

Forbes, David W. 1992a. *Encounters With Paradise: Views of Hawaii and Its People, 1778–1941.* Honolulu: Honolulu Academy of Arts.

——. 1992b. *Treasures of Hawaiian History.* Honolulu: Hawaiian Historical Society.

Frear, Mary Dillingham. 1934. *Lowell and Abigail, A Realistic Idyll.* New Haven, CT: Privately printed.

Furumoto, Augustine S., N. Norby Nielsen, and William R. Phillips. 1972. *A Study of Past Earthquakes, Isoseismic Zones of Intensity and Recommended Zones for Structural Design for Hawaii.* Honolulu: University of Hawaii, Center for Engineering Research.

Gadd, Mike, John Boothroyd, and Ann Durrell. 1980. *The Book of Windsurfing, A Guide to Freesailing Techniques.* Toronto, New York, Cincinnati, London, and Melbourne: Van Nostrand Reinhold Ltd.

Gast, Ross H., and Agnes C. Conrad. 1973. *Don Francisco de Paula Marin.* Honolulu: University Press of Hawai'i, for the Hawaiian Historical Society.

Gibbs, Jim. 1977. *Shipwrecks in Paradise: An Informal Marine History of the Hawaiian Islands.* Seattle: Superior Publishing Co.

Glick, Clarence C. 1980. *Sojourners and Settlers: Chinese Migrants to Hawaii.* Honolulu: Hawaii Chinese History Center and University of Hawai'i Press.

Greer, Richard A. 1966. *Downtown Profile: Honolulu A Century Ago.* Honolulu: The Kamehameha Schools Press.

Gutmanis, June. 1977. *Kahuna La'au Lapa'au, The Practice of Hawaiian Herbal Medicine.* Honolulu: Island Heritage.

Haar, Francis, and Prithwish Neogy. 1974. *Artists of Hawaii.* Vol. one. Honolulu: The State Foundation on Culture & the Arts and University Press of Hawai'i.

Hackler, Rhoda E. A. 1982. *Royal Portraits of Hawaii.* Honolulu: The Friends of Iolani Palace.

——. 1987. *'Iolani Palace.* Honolulu: Friends of Iolani Palace.

Halford, Francis John, M.D. 1954. *9 Doctors & God.* Honolulu: University of Hawai'i Press.

Hall, David. 1948. *The Record Book, International Edition.* Reprint 1978. Westport, CT: Greenwood.

Hall, Major. 1985. *Sports Illustrated Boardsailing*. New York: Harper & Row.

Handy, E. S. Craighill, and Kenneth P. Emory, Edwin H. Bryan, Peter H. Buck, John H. Wise, and others. 1965. *Ancient Hawaiian Civilization*. Rutland, VT, and Tokyo: Charles E. Tuttle Co.

——, and Mary Kawena Pukui. 1972. *The Polynesian Family System in Ka'u, Hawaii*. Rutland, VT, and Tokyo: Charles E. Tuttle Co.

Hardy, D. Elmo. 1960. *Insects of Hawaii*. Vol. 10. Honolulu: University of Hawai'i Press.

Hibbard, Don, and David Franzen. 1986. *The View From Diamond Head*. Honolulu: Editions Limited.

Hiroa, Te Rangi (Peter H. Buck). 1957. *Arts and Crafts of Hawaii*. Honolulu: Bernice Pauahi Bishop Museum Press.

Historic Buildings Task Force. 1969. *Old Honolulu*. Honolulu: Historic Buildings Task Force.

Hitch, Thomas K., and Mary Ishii Kuramoto. 1981. *Waialae Country Club, The First Half Century*. Honolulu: Waialae Country Club.

Hodge, Clarence L., and Peggy Ferris. 1950. *Building Honolulu*. Honolulu: Chamber of Commerce of Honolulu.

Ii, John Papa. 1983. *Fragments of Hawaiian History*. Translated by Mary Kawena Pukui. Revised edition. Honolulu: Bernice Pauahi Bishop Museum Press.

Jenkins, Irving. 1983. *Hawaiian Furniture and Hawaii's Cabinet Makers 1820–1940*. Honolulu: Published for the Daughters of Hawaii by Editions Limited.

Joesting, Edward. 1983. *Tides of Commerce*. Honolulu: First Hawaiian, Inc.

Johannessen, Edward. 1956. *The Hawaiian Labor Movement: A Brief History*. Boston: Bruce Humphries, Inc.

Johnson, Donald D. 1991. *The City and County of Honolulu, A Government Chronicle*. Honolulu: University of Hawai'i Press and City Council of the City and County of Honolulu.

Judd, Bernice, Janet E. Bell, and Clare G. Murdoch. Comp. 1978. *Hawaiian Language Imprints, 1822–1899*. Honolulu: HMCS and University Press of Hawai'i.

Judd, Walter F. 1975. *Palaces and Forts of the Hawaiian Kingdom*. Palo Alto, CA: Pacific Books.

Kamins, Robert M. 1952. *The Tax System of Hawaii*. Honolulu: University of Hawai'i Press.

Kanahele, George S., ed. 1979. *Hawaiian Music and Musicians*. Honolulu: University of Hawai'i Press.

Kane, Joseph Nathan. 1981. *Famous First Facts*. Fourth edition. New York: H. W. Wilson.

Kirch, Patrick Vinton. 1985. *Feathered Gods and Fishhooks: An Introduction to Hawaiian Archaeology and Prehistory*. Honolulu: University of Hawai'i Press.

Kobayashi, Victor N., ed. 1983. *Building a Rainbow*. Honolulu: Hui O Students, University of Hawai'i at Mānoa.

Krauss, Bob. 1988. *Keneti: South Seas Adventures of Kenneth Emory*. Honolulu: University of Hawai'i Press.

Kuykendall, Ralph S. 1938. *The Hawaiian Kingdom*, Vol. 1, *1778–1854, Foundation and Transformation*. Honolulu: University of Hawai'i Press.

——. 1953. *The Hawaiian Kingdom*, Vol. 2, *1854–1874, Twenty Critical Years*. Honolulu: University of Hawai'i Press.

———. 1967. *The Hawaiian Kingdom*, Vol. 3, *1874–1893, The Kalakaua Dynasty*. Honolulu: University of Hawai'i Press.

———, and A. Grove Day. 1961. *Hawaii: A History*. Englewood Cliffs, NJ: Prentice-Hall, Inc.

Loomis, Albertine. 1976. *For Whom Are the Stars*. Honolulu: University of Hawai'i Press and Friends of the Library of Hawaii.

Lord, Walter. 1957. *Day of Infamy*. New York: Holt, Rinehart and Winston.

Lueras, Leonard. 1984. *Surfing, the Ultimate Pleasure*. Hong Kong and Honolulu: Emphasis International Ltd.

Lum, Arlene, ed. 1988. *Sailing for the Sun, The Chinese in Hawaii 1789–1989*. Honolulu: Three Heroes.

Luomala, Katharine. 1984. *Hula Ki'i, Hawaiian Puppetry*. Laie, HI.: Brigham Young University–Hawai'i Campus.

Lyman, Henry, M.D. 1906. *Hawaiian Yesterdays*. Chicago: A. C. McClurg & Co.

Macdonald, Gordon A., Agatin T. Abbott, and Frank L. Peterson. 1983. *Volcanoes in the Sea*. Second edition. Honolulu: University of Hawai'i Press.

Malo, David. 1951. *Hawaiian Antiquities*. Second edition. Translated by N. B. Emerson. Honolulu: Bernice Pauahi Bishop Museum, Special Publication 2.

Mazlish, Bruce, and Edwin Diamond. 1979. *Jimmy Carter, A Character Portrait*. New York: Simon & Schuster.

McDole, Katherine D. 1962. *Iamei i Hiki Ai. It Happened in Hawaii*. Honolulu: Privately printed.

McKeown, Sean. 1978. *Hawaiian Reptiles and Amphibians*. Honolulu: Oriental Publishing Co.

Meyen, F. J. 1981. *A Botanist's Visit to Oahu in 1831*. Translated by Astrid Jackson. Kailua, O'ahu: Press Pacifica.

Meyer, Henry A., et al. 1948. *Hawaii, Its Stamps and Postal History*. New York, The Philatelic Foundation.

Morley, Sheridan. 1969. *A Talent to Amuse*. Garden City, NY: Doubleday and Co.

Mulholland, John F. 1970. *Hawaii's Religions*. Rutland, VT, and Tokyo: Charles E. Tuttle Co.

Myatt, Carl. 1991. *Hawaii, The Electric Century*. Honolulu: Signature Publishing for Hawaiian Electric Co.

Neal, Marie C. 1965. *In Gardens of Hawaii*. Revised edition. Honolulu: Bernice Pauahi Bishop Museum Press.

Neft, David S., and Richard M. Cohen. 1985. *The Sports Encyclopedia: Baseball*. Sixth edition. New York: St. Martin's Press.

Nellist, George F. M., ed. 1941. *Pan-Pacific Who's Who, 1940–41 Edition*. Honolulu: Honolulu Star-Bulletin, Ltd.

———, ed. 1925. *The Story of Hawaii and Its Builders*. Honolulu: Honolulu Star-Bulletin, Ltd.

———, ed. c. 1938. *Women of Hawaii*. Vol. 2. Honolulu: E. A. Langton-Boyle.

Nordyke, Eleanor C. 1989. *The Peopling of Hawaii*. Second edition. Honolulu: University of Hawai'i Press.

Ogawa, Dennis M., and Glen Grant. 1986. *Ellison S. Onizuka: A Remembrance*. Honolulu: Signature/Mutual Publishing of Honolulu.

Panati, Charles. 1987. *Extraordinary Origins of Everyday Things*. New York: Harper & Row.

Patterson, Wayne. 1988. *The Korean Frontier in America: Immigration to Hawaii, 1896–1910.* Honolulu: University of Hawai'i Press.

Petersen, William. 1969. *Population.* Second edition. Toronto: Collier Macmillan.

Peterson, Barbara Bennett, ed. 1984. *Notable Women of Hawaii.* Honolulu: University of Hawai'i Press.

Philipp, Perry F. 1953. *Diversified Agriculture of Hawaii.* Honolulu: University of Hawai'i Press.

Prange, Gordon W. 1986. *Pearl Harbor: The Verdict of History.* New York: McGraw-Hill Book Co.

Pukui, Mary Kawena, and Samuel Elbert. 1986. *Hawaiian Dictionary.* Revised edition. Honolulu: University of Hawai'i Press.

Reichler, Joseph L., ed. 1982. *The Baseball Encyclopedia.* Fifth edition. New York: Macmillan Publishing Co.

Robertson, Patrick. 1974. *The Book of Firsts.* New York: Clarkson Potter.

Ronck, Ronn. 1984. *Ronck's Hawaii Almanac.* Honolulu: University of Hawai'i Press.

Rose, G. Roger. 1980. *A Museum to Instruct and Delight: William T. Brigham and the Founding of Bernice Pauahi Bishop Museum.* Honolulu: Bernice Pauahi Bishop Museum Press.

Sandoz, Philip. 1992. *Sumo Showdown, The Hawaiian Challenge.* Rutland, VT, and Tokyo: Charles E. Tuttle Co.

Schmitt, Robert C. 1968. *Demographic Statistics of Hawaii: 1778–1965.* Honolulu: University of Hawai'i Press.

———. 1973. *The Missionary Censuses of Hawaii.* Pacific Anthropological Records, No. 20. Honolulu: Bernice Pauahi Bishop Museum, Department of Anthropology.

———. 1977. *Historical Statistics of Hawaii.* Honolulu: University Press of Hawai'i.

———. 1988. *Hawaii in the Movies: 1898–1959.* Honolulu: Hawaiian Historical Society.

Scott, Edward B. 1968. *The Saga of the Sandwich Islands.* Crystal Bay, NV: Sierra-Tahoe.

Shigeura, Gordon T., and Hiroshi Ooka. 1984. *Macadamia Nuts in Hawaii: History and Production.* Honolulu: University of Hawai'i, College of Tropical Agriculture and Human Resources, Research Extension Series 039.

Silverman, Jane L. 1987. *Kaahumanu, Molder of Change.* Honolulu: Friends of the Judiciary History Center of Hawaii.

Simmons, Dawn Langley. 1979. *Rosalynn Carter, Her Life Story.* New York: Frederick Fell Publishers, Inc.

Simonds, William H. 1958. *The Hawaiian Telephone Story.* Honolulu: Hawaiian Telephone Co.

Simpson, Sir George. 1847. *Narrative of a Journey Round the World, During the Years 1841 and 1842.* Three volumes. London: Henry Colburn.

Smock, Jack. 1980. *Transpac.* San Diego: The Transpacific Yacht Club and the Maritime Museums Association of San Diego.

Stannard, David E. 1989. *Before the Horror: The Population of Hawai'i on the Eve of Western Contact.* Honolulu: Social Science Research Institute, University of Hawai'i.

State of Hawai'i. 1967–. *The State of Hawaii Data Book: A Statistical Abstract.* Published annually (except 1969). Honolulu: Hawaii State Department of Business, Economic

Development & Tourism and its predecessor agencies, the Department of Planning & Economic Development and the Department of Business & Economic Development.

Steele, H. Thomas. 1984. *The Hawaiian Shirt, Its Art and History.* New York: Abbeville Press.

Stewart, C. S. 1970. *Journal of a Residence in the Sandwich Islands.* . . Facsimile reprint of the third edition of 1830. Honolulu: University of Hawai'i Press, for Friends of the Library of Hawaii.

Takaki, Ronald. 1983. *Pau Hana.* Honolulu: University of Hawai'i Press.

Thomas, Mifflin K. 1985. *Schooner from Windward.* Honolulu: University of Hawai'i Press.

Thurston, Lorrin, ed. 1904. *The Fundamental Law of Hawaii.* Honolulu: The Hawaiian Gazette Co., Ltd.

Tilton, Cecil G. 1927. *The History of Banking in Hawaii.* Honolulu: University of Hawai'i, Research Publications No. 3.

Tomich, P. Quentin. 1986. *Mammals in Hawaii.* Second edition. Honolulu: Bernice Pauahi Bishop Museum Press.

Turkin, Hy, and S. C. Thompson. 1977. *The Official Encyclopedia of Baseball.* South Brunswick and New York: A. S. Barnes & Co.

United Japanese Society of Hawaii. 1971. *A History of Japanese in Hawaii.* Honolulu: The United Japanese Society of Hawaii.

Van Dyke, Robert E., and Ronn Ronck. 1982. *Hawaiian Yesterdays: Historical Photographs by Ray Jerome Baker.* Honolulu: Mutual Publishing Co.

Wang, Jim. 1982. *Hawaii State and Local Politics.* Hilo: James C. F. Wang.

Whipple, A. B. C. 1973. *Yankee Whalers in the South Seas.* Rutland, VT, and Tokyo: Charles E. Tuttle Co.

Whitman, John B. 1979. *An Account of the Sandwich Islands. The Hawaiian Journal of John B. Whitman, 1813–1815.* Edited by John Dominis Holt. Honolulu: Topgallant Publishing Co., Ltd.; and Salem, MA: Peabody Museum of Salem.

Whitney, Henry M. 1875. *The Hawaiian Guide Book.* Honolulu: Henry M. Whitney.

———. 1890. *The Tourists' Guide Through the Hawaiian Islands.* Honolulu: The Hawaiian Gazette Co.

Wilder, Kinau. 1978. *Wilders of Waikiki.* Honolulu: Topgallant Publishing Co., Ltd.

Williams, Francis X. 1931. *Handbook of the Insects and Other Invertebrates of Hawaiian Sugar Cane Fields.* Honolulu: Experiment Station of the Hawaiian Sugar Planters' Association.

Wist, Benjamin O. 1940. *A Century of Public Education in Hawaii.* Honolulu: Hawaii Educational Review.

Works Progress Administration. n.d. *A Classified Directory of Business, Governmental, Educational and Professional Activities on Oahu, Hawaii (As of October 31, 1936).* Honolulu: Industrial and Commercial Survey Project of the W.P.A., cooperating with the Chamber of Commerce of Honolulu. Typescript, AH.

Young, Nat, with Craig McGregor. 1983. *The History of Surfing.* Palm Beach, New South Wales, Australia: Palm Beach Press.

Yzendoorn, Father Reginald. 1927. *History of the Catholic Mission in the Hawaiian Islands.* Honolulu Star-Bulletin, Ltd.

Zimmerman, Elwood C. *Insects of Hawaii.* Vol. 2 (1948), Vol. 7 (1958). Honolulu: University of Hawai'i Press.

Articles by
Robert C. Schmitt

The following articles by Robert C. Schmitt may provide more detailed information and footnotes on the Hawaii "firsts" included in this book. The information in *Firsts and Almost Firsts in Hawaii*, however, should be considered the most accurate and up-to-date.

"Hawaii's First Hospitals," *HMJ*, vol. 8, no. 6, July-August 1949, pp. 424–427.

"Little Greenwich: Hawaii's First Hospital," *PP*, vol. 61, no. 12, December 1949, pp. 38–40.

"Hawaii's Hospitals, 1831–1956," *HMJ*, vol. 15, no. 4, March-April 1956, pp. 338–341.

"From Umi to UNIVAC: Data Processing in Hawaii, 1500–1965," *Seventy-Fourth Annual Report of the Hawaiian Historical Society for the Year 1965*, 1966, pp. 17–28. Updated version, without footnotes, published as "Data Processing in Hawaii, 1500–1980," *The Printout*, vol. 2, no. 5, May 15, 1980, pp. 19, 27, and vol. 2, no. 6, June 15, 1980, pp. 6–7, 28.

"Early Crime Statistics of Hawaii," *HHR*, vol. 2, no. 4, July 1966, pp. 325–332.

"Hawaii's First Phonographs," *HHR*, vol. 2, no. 8, July 1967, pp. 394–395.

"Notes on Hawaiian Photography Before 1890," *HHR*, vol. 2, no. 9, October 1967, pp. 409–416.

"Movies in Hawaii, 1897–1932," *HJH*, vol. 1, 1967, pp. 73–82. Reprinted, with corrections, in *Out-takes* (Hawaii Film Board), Winter 1981, pp. 1, 13–18.

"Automobile Ownership in Hawaii Before 1931: Dates and Data," *HHR*, vol. 2, no. 10, January 1968, pp. 426–432.

"South Sea Movies, 1913–1943," *HHR*, vol. 2, no. 11, April 1968, pp. 433–452 (entire issue).

"The Day the Movies Came to Old Hawaii," *H*, vol. 3, no. 9, March 1969, pp. 6–9.

"Population Policy in Hawaii," *HJH*, vol. 8, 1974, pp. 90–110.

"Some Firsts in Island Leisure," *HJH*, vol. 12, 1978, pp. 99–119.

"Some Transportation and Communication Firsts in Hawaii," *HJH*, vol. 13, 1979, pp. 99–123.

"Some Firsts in Island Business and Government," *HJH*, vol. 14, 1980, pp. 80–108.

"Famous First Words," *Paradise News*, May 1981, pp. 1, 6.

"Historic Hawaiian Bridges," *HHN*, vol. 7, no. 9, October 1981, pp. 4–5.

"Health and Medical Firsts in Hawaii," *HMJ*, vol. 40, no. 10, October 1981, pp. 284–289.

"Some Construction and Housing Firsts in Hawaii," *HJH*, vol. 15, 1981, pp. 100–112.

"Pipes, Pools, and Privies: Some Notes on Early Island Plumbing," *HJH*, vol. 16, 1982, pp. 149–170.

"Royal Crowns and Historic Plaque: Dentistry in Hawaii During the 19th Century," *HJH*, vol. 17, 1983, pp. 143–155.

"Two Centuries of Eye Care in Hawai'i," *HJH*, vol. 19, 1985, pp. 134–148.

"Hawaii's First Ophthalmologist," *HMJ*, vol. 45, no. 9, September 1986, pp. 323–324.

"Early Hawaiian Bridges," *HJH*, vol. 20, 1986, pp. 151–157.

"Survey Research in Hawaii Before 1950," *HJH*, vol. 21, 1987, pp. 110–125.

"Some 'Firsts' That Weren't," *HJH*, vol. 21, 1987, pp. 156–157.

"Hawaii's First Fax," *H*, vol. 27, no. 4, October 1992, p. 22.

"Hawaiian Time," *HJH*, vol. 26, 1992, pp. 207–225. With Doak C. Cox.

"More 'Firsts' That Weren't," *HJH*, vol. 27, 1993, pp. 239–244.

"Early Island Conventions," *HJH*, vol. 28, 1994, pp. 109–111.

"Some Notes on Censorship in Hawaii before 1950," *HJH*, vol. 28, 1994, pp. 157–161.